Blackstone's

Police Q&A

Evidence and Procedure 2017

Blackstone's
Police Q&A

Evidence and Procedure 2017

Fifteenth edition

Huw Smart and John Watson

OXFORD
UNIVERSITY PRESS

OXFORD
UNIVERSITY PRESS

Great Clarendon Street, Oxford, OX2 6DP,
United Kingdom

Oxford University Press is a department of the University of Oxford.
It furthers the University's objective of excellence in research, scholarship,
and education by publishing worldwide. Oxford is a registered trade mark of
Oxford University Press in the UK and in certain other countries

First published in 2016

Impression: 1

Published in the United States of America by Oxford University Press
198 Madison Avenue, New York, NY 10016, United States of America

British Library Cataloguing in Publication Data
Data available

ISBN 978-0-19-878311-4

Printed and bound by
CPI Group (UK) Ltd, Croydon, CR0 4YY

Contents

Contents

Introduction

Before you get into the detail of this book, there are two myths about multiple-choice questions (MCQs) that we need to get out of the way right at the start:

1. that they are easy to answer;
2. that they are easy to write.

Take one look at a professionally designed and properly developed exam paper such as those used by the Police Promotion Examinations Board or the National Board of Medical Examiners in the US and the first myth collapses straight away. Contrary to what some people believe, MCQs are not an easy solution for examiners and not a 'multiple-guess' soft option for examinees.

That is not to say that all MCQs are taxing, or even testing—in the psychometric sense. If MCQs are to have any real value at all, they need to be carefully designed and follow some agreed basic rules.

And this leads us to myth number 2.

It is widely assumed by many people and educational organisations that anyone with the knowledge of a subject can write MCQs. You need only look at how few MCQ writing courses are offered by training providers in the UK to see just how far this myth is believed. Similarly, you need only to have a go at a few badly designed MCQs to realise that it is a myth nonetheless. Writing bad MCQs is easy; writing good ones is no easier than answering them!

As with many things, the design of MCQs benefits considerably from time, training and experience. Many MCQ writers fall easily and often unwittingly into the trap of making their questions too hard, too easy or too obscure, or completely different from the type of question that you will eventually encounter in your own particular exam. Others seem to use the MCQ as a way to catch people out or to show how smart they, the authors, are (or think they are).

There are several purposes for which MCQs are very useful. The first is in producing a reliable, valid and fair test of knowledge and understanding across a wide range of subject matter. Another is an aid to study, preparation and revision for such examinations and tests. The differences in objective mean that there are slight differences in the rules that the MCQ writers follow. Whereas the design of fully validated MCQs to be used in high stakes examinations which will effectively determine who passes and who fails have very strict guidelines as to construction, content and style, less stringent rules apply to MCQs that are being used for teaching and revision. For that reason, there may be types of MCQ that are appropriate in the latter setting which would not be used in the former. However, in developing the MCQs for this book, the authors have tried to follow the fundamental rules of MCQ design but they would not claim to have replicated the level of psychometric rigour that is—and has to be—adopted by the type of examining bodies referred to previously.

These MCQs are designed to reinforce your knowledge and understanding, to highlight any gaps or weaknesses in that knowledge and understanding and to help focus your revision of the relevant topics.

I hope that we have achieved that aim.

Good luck!

Blackstone's Police Q&As—Special Features

References to Blackstone's Police Manuals

Every answer is followed by a paragraph reference to Blackstone's Police Manuals. This means that once you have attempted a question and looked at an answer, the Manual can immediately be referred to for help and clarification.

Unique numbers for each question

Each question and answer has the same unique number. This should ensure that there is no confusion as to which question is linked to which answer. For example, Question 2.1 is linked to Answer 2.1.

Checklists

The checklists are designed to help you keep track of your progress when answering the multiple-choice questions. If you fill in the checklist after attempting a question, you will be able to check how many you got right on the first attempt and will know immediately which questions need to be revisited a second time. Please visit www.blackstonespoliceservice.com and click through to the Blackstone's Police Q&As 2017 page. You will then find electronic versions of the checklists to download and print out. Email any queries or comments on the book to: police.uk@oup.com.

Acknowledgements

This book has been written as an accompaniment to Blackstone's Police Manuals, and will test the knowledge you have accrued through reading that series. It is of the essence that full study of the relevant chapters in each Police Manual is completed prior to attempting the Questions and Answers. As qualified police trainers we recognise that students tend to answer questions incorrectly either because they don't read the question properly, or because one of the 'distracters' has done its work. The distracter is one of the three incorrect answers in an MCQ, and is designed to distract you from the correct answer, and in this way discriminate between candidates: the better-prepared candidate not being 'distracted'.

So particular attention should be paid to the *Answers* sections and students should ask themselves, 'Why did I get that question wrong?' and, just as importantly, 'Why did I get that question right?' Combining the information gained in the *Answers* section together with re-reading the chapter in the Police Manuals should lead to a greater understanding of the subject matter.

The authors wish to thank all the staff at Oxford University Press who have helped put this publication together. We would particularly like to dedicate these books to Alistair McQueen who sadly passed away in 2008. It was his vision and support that got this project off the ground. Without his help neither Huw nor John would have been able to make these Q&As the success they are. We would also like to show appreciation to Fraser Sampson, former consultant editor of Blackstone's Police Manuals, whose influence on these Q&As is appreciated.

Huw would like to thank Caroline for her constant love, support and understanding over the past year—and her ability to withstand the pressures of being the partner to a workaholic! Special thanks to Lawrence and Maddie—two perfect young adults. Last but not least, love and special affection to Haf and Nia, two beautiful young girls.

John would like to thank Sue, David, Catherine and Andrew for their continued support through long hours sat in front of the computer.

1 | Sources of Law and the Courts

STUDY PREPARATION

This chapter examines what could be best described as the building blocks of criminal law, the body of laws; common, statutory and delegated legislation. This chapter also examines what are known as 'precedents' or the details of cases that have been 'decided' in the higher courts and the impact these have on current and future cases. Students should recognise that what they have erroneously called 'stated cases' for years are probably not 'stated'. But more importantly, they should recognise the importance of these authorities, not just in their working lives as police officers, but as students of the law in any capacity; particularly candidates for promotion.

Then building on how laws are made we look at how the law is decided and interpreted in the courts.

The nature of an offence will determine in which court a case is heard. In England and Wales offences can be tried in either the magistrates' court or the Crown Court. Offences committed by a child or young person are generally heard in the youth court.

This chapter also tests your knowledge of the categories of offences and the criminal courts where these are dealt with.

QUESTIONS

Question 1.1

Common law is still very much part of modern law, and it is still commanding legislation.

As a whole, where do its sources lie?

A Principles of the law declared by the judges in the course of deciding particular cases.

B Principles of the law declared by High Court judges in the course of deciding particular cases.

C Principles of the law declared by the most senior law courts in the course of deciding particular cases.

D Principles of the law that have evolved over time.

Question 1.2

STRUTHERS is appearing at Crown Court charged with robbery, and has been convicted at Crown Court. His barrister was successful in gaining an acquittal on a point of law following appeal to the Court of Appeal. The High Court judge also commented that the police action in obtaining witness evidence had been on the point of being unlawful.

Which of the following is true in relation to precedent?

A In future cases lower courts will have to follow the point of law made by the High Court judge.

B In future cases lower courts will have to follow the point of law, and the comments made by the High Court judge about the police action.

C In future cases lower courts will have to follow the point of law, and the comments made by the High Court judge about the police action, but only if it is the same police officers.

D The decision is not binding on lower courts as it was not a judgment laid down by the Law Lords in the Supreme Court.

Question 1.3

DAVIES has been charged with shoplifting—the value of the theft was £50; DAVIES has many previous convictions for theft. The court is considering the mode of trial of DAVIES in respect of this latest theft.

In relation to this which of the following is correct?

A Due to the value of the theft this is a summary only offence and DAVIES cannot elect trial by jury.

B Due to the value of the theft this is a summary only offence but DAVIES can elect trial by jury.

C Theft is an either-way offence irrespective of value and DAVIES can elect trial by jury.

D As DAVIES has previous convictions, if the court feels a custodial sentence is appropriate it must be sent to the Crown Court for trial.

Question 1.4

BRIAN is an 11-year-old boy who is appearing at the youth court on a charge of causing or inciting a boy under the age of 13 to engage in sexual activity of a non-penetrative nature contrary to s. 8(1) and (3) of the Sexual Offences Act 2003. BRIAN has no previous convictions and is of good character.

In relation to this should BRIAN be sent to the Crown Court for trial?

A Yes, this would be considered a 'grave' offence and should be sent to the Crown Court for trial.

B Yes, as this is a specified offence under s. 224 of the Criminal Justice Act 2003 it must be sent to the Crown Court for trial.

C No, not unless the magistrate felt there was a real prospect that the Crown Court would impose a custodial sentence.

D No, as the youth has no previous convictions and is of good character the case should be tried in the youth court.

Question 1.5

A young woman is appearing before a youth court on a charge of theft. There are only two lay magistrates available and neither are female.

Can the trial proceed in these circumstances?

A Yes, provided both magistrates agree *in camera* to proceed after hearing submissions from all the parties.

B Yes, provided both magistrates agree in open court to proceed after hearing submissions from all the parties.

C No, in all cases where there are only two magistrates the bench must include both a man and a woman.

D No, in cases involving a female young person the bench must include both a man and a woman.

Question 1.6

At the Court of Appeal a High Court judge has given a ruling in relation to a point of law raised by the defence in an attempt to stay proceedings. The judge gave directions in relation to principles of law and also gives an opinion on some connected matter.

Which of the following is correct in relation to the 'opinion' the judge gave?

A This 'opinion' is called *ratio decidendi* and is binding on lower courts.

B This 'opinion' is called *ratio decidendi* and may be persuasive, but not binding on lower courts.

C This 'opinion' is called *obiter dictum* and is binding on lower courts.

D This 'opinion' is called *obiter dictum* and may be persuasive, but not binding on lower courts.

Question 1.7

GRIFFITHS has been charged with an indictable sexual offence. He fears a hefty jail sentence and wishes the matter to be held in the magistrates' court. He has indicated that he intends to plead not guilty.

Which of the following will the magistrates' court consider to determine the mode of trial?

A The seriousness of the offence only.

B The seriousness of the offence, and the defendant's previous convictions.

C The seriousness of the offence, the defendant's previous convictions, and assessing whether their powers of punishment are sufficient.

D The seriousness of the offence, the defendant's previous convictions, and the number of witnesses in the case.

Question 1.8

HELPS is appearing before the magistrates' court for the offence of carrying an insecure load, contrary to reg. 100(2) of the Road Vehicles (Construction and Use) Regulations 1986 and s. 42 of the Road Traffic Act 1988. He has received a computer-generated requisition as a result of a written charge.

The date of the alleged offence was 16 June. The information date printed at the head of the requisition was 10 December; that is six days before the effluxion of the six months' limitation period. The summons, which was dated 9 January, included a statement of facts. It also bore the date when the information was printed, 20 December; that is, four days outside the limit.

Bearing in mind this discrepancy in 'information' dates in the requisition, which of the following is correct as to whether the information was laid in time?

A The date at the top should be accepted as correct, as it was computer-generated information.

B It is for the defence to prove, on the balance of probabilities, that it was *not* laid in time.

C It is for the magistrates to decide if it was laid in time, applying the criminal standard of proof.

D It is for the Clerk of the Court to decide if it was laid in time, on the balance of probabilities.

Question 1.9

GRUNDY is 17 years of age and will be 18 in one month's time; he is appearing at youth court charged with rape and the court is considering whether it should deal with the matter or whether to send GRUNDY to Crown Court to be tried.

Which of the following is correct?

A As GRUNDY is not yet 18 he must be tried and sentenced in the youth court.

B He must be sent to Crown Court as he will be 18 by the time he stands trial.

C He can be tried in the youth court for this offence at the discretion on the magistrates, but can be sent to Crown Court for sentence.

D Given the sentence for rape he must be sent to the Crown Court for trial.

Question 1.10

DICKENS is appearing at magistrates' court on two counts of theft. He has been found guilty and the bench is considering sentence. Theft is an offence that is triable either way.

What is the maximum sentence that can be imposed by the magistrates?

A 6 months for each which must run concurrently.

B 6 months for each which must run consecutively.

C 12 months for each which must run concurrently.

D 12 months for each which must run consecutively.

Question 1.11

DAWLISH is a youth aged 16 who has been charged with an offence of allowing a child death. He is appearing at the youth court and wishes to elect trial by jury at the Crown Court.

In relation to this which of the following is correct?

A As he is 16 years of age he must be tried and sentenced in the youth court.

B Irrespective of his age he may elect to be tried in the Crown Court or the youth court due to being charged with a serious offence.

C As he is 16 years of age and charged with an offence of allowing a child death he may elect to be tried in the Crown Court or the youth court.

D As he is charged with an offence of allowing a child death offence he will be sent directly to the Crown Court for trial, he has no option.

Question 1.12

HIGGINS is appearing before the magistrates' court having never been in a court before. He asks his solicitor who will be hearing the case and if they are legally qualified.

In relation to this, which of the following is correct?

A Three lay magistrates, none of whom need be legally qualified.

B Three lay magistrates, one of whom has to be legally qualified.

C At least two lay magistrates, neither of whom need be legally qualified.

D At least two lay magistrates sitting with a single district judge.

Question 1.13

BLAKELY is a District Judge who has been subject to several legal challenges and has had a significant number of his decisions overturned by the Queen's Bench Division of the High Court. Local solicitors consider that the justices' clerk is not providing good advice.

Which of the following is correct?

A A justices' clerk is not legally qualified and cannot provide advice.

B The justices' clerk cannot provide legal advice to a district judge.

C A justices' clerk can give legal advice to a district judge.

D A justices' clerk can give advice only on procedure and practice.

Question 1.14

JEAVONS is aged 17 years and is appearing before the youth court; the district judge asks JEAVONS to confirm if his parents are there and he states that they won't be coming as they 'can't be bothered anymore'.

In relation to any power to order the parents to attend the proceedings in the youth court, which of the following is correct?

A Only as it is a district judge and not a lay bench sitting is there power to order the parents to attend the proceedings.

B The youth court has the power to order JEAVONS's parent or guardian to attend the proceedings and *must* make such an order.

C The youth court has the power to order JEAVONS's parent or guardian to attend the proceedings and *may* make such an order.

D The youth court has *no* power to order JEAVONS's parent or guardian to attend the proceedings as he is not aged under 16.

Question 1.15

A serving police officer has been called to jury service and is awaiting selection. One of the trials about to go ahead contains contentious police evidence and the court is considering whether the police officer should sit on this jury.

In relation to this which of the following is correct?

A The officer should not sit on this jury unless absolutely necessary.

B The officer should not sit on this jury in any circumstances.

C The officer should only sit on this jury with the express approval of the trial judge.

D The officer can sit on the jury; there is no reason why they cannot.

Question 1.16

There are restrictions in relation to qualification for jury service with regard to someone who has been ordinarily resident in the United Kingdom, the Channel Islands or the Isle of Man.

Which of the following is correct?

A Resident for any period of at least five years since attaining the age of 13.

B Resident for any period of at least seven years since attaining the age of 11.

C Resident for any period of at least five years until reaching 18 years of age.

D Resident for any period of at least seven years until reaching 18 years of age.

ANSWERS

Answer 1.1

Answer **A** — There is no authoritative text of the common law and, as a whole, its sources lie in the principles of the law declared by the judges in the course of deciding particular cases; answers B, C and D are therefore incorrect. It should be noted that the common law can only be declared authoritatively by the judge(s) of the superior courts (i.e. from the High Court), and then only to the extent that it is necessary to do so for the purpose of deciding a particular case. For this reason, the development of the common law has always been dependent upon the incidence of cases arising for decision, and the particular facts of those cases.

Evidence and Procedure, para. 2.1.2

Answer 1.2

Answer **A** — The system of courts in England and Wales is a hierarchy, the various courts being related to one another as superior and inferior. An inferior court is generally bound by the decision and directions of a superior court. For example, judges of the Divisional Court and Crown Courts are bound by the decisions of the Court of Appeal; answer D is therefore incorrect. It should be noted that, although the Crown Court is superior to a magistrates' court and enjoys wider powers, it is still a 'lower' court and its decisions are not generally binding on other courts.

When it is said that a decision is binding and authoritative precedent, what is meant is that the principle of law on which the decision was based, or the reason for the decision, is binding. This principle of the law is known as the *ratio decidendi* of the case. An example of this would be the decision that, once the prosecution have proved that a defendant was carrying a weapon that is 'offensive' *per se*, there is no need to prove any intention to use that weapon offensively.

The *ratio decidendi* consists only of the principle(s) of law essential to a decision. A judge, or court as a whole, may sometimes go beyond the facts of a particular case and give an opinion on some connected matter which is intended to be of guidance in future cases. Such an opinion is known as an *obiter dictum*, and may be persuasive, but not binding, on other courts in a future case, even if the same parties are involved; answers B and C are therefore incorrect.

Evidence and Procedure, para. 2.1.4.1

Answer 1.3

Answer **B** — Where a person aged over 18 is charged with an offence that is triable either way, the magistrates' court convenes a mode of trial hearing.

If a defendant pleads not guilty or has not indicated an intention to plead guilty to an offence triable either way, a magistrates' court must decide whether the offence is more suitable for summary trial or trial on indictment (Magistrates' Courts Act 1980, s. 19).

Generally speaking, theft is an either-way offence, however, s. 22A of the Magistrates' Courts Act 1980 relates to low-value shoplifting and provides that, where the value of the stolen goods does not exceed £200, the offence is triable only summarily; answer C is therefore incorrect. That said, under s. 22A(2) a person must nonetheless be allowed to elect trial in the Crown Court; answer A is therefore incorrect.

If a magistrates' court feel a custodial sentence is appropriate they can impose one within statutory limitations; only where those limitations are restrictive should the case be remitted to the Crown Court for sentence; answer D is therefore incorrect.

Evidence and Procedure, para. 2.1.6.4

Answer 1.4

Answer **C** — The general principle is that persons under the age of 18 years should be tried and sentenced in the youth court for both summary and indictable offences. Sections 51 and 51A of the Crime and Disorder Act 1998 deal with those cases where a juvenile must be tried on indictment or the magistrates have a discretion to send a juvenile to the Crown Court for trial. Section 51A(2) and (3) require the magistrates' court to send juveniles directly to the Crown Court for trial where they are charged with:

(a) homicide; or
(b) a firearms offence where there is a mandatory minimum sentence (Firearms Act 1968, s. 51A), or an offence under the Violent Crime Reduction Act 2006, s. 29(3) (minimum sentences in certain cases of using someone to mind a weapon);
(c) an offence to which the provisions of s. 91 of the Powers of Criminal Courts (Sentencing) Act 2000 apply and the court considers that it ought to be possible to sentence the juvenile to detention under that section in the event of his being convicted of the offence; or
(d) the offence is a 'specified offence' (under the Criminal Justice Act 2003, s. 224) and it appears to the court that, if he is found guilty of the offence, the criteria for the imposition of a sentence under s. 226B of the Criminal Justice Act 2003 (extended sentence for certain violent or sexual offences) would be met (this makes it more than just a specified offence and answer B is therefore incorrect).

Trials of juveniles in the Crown Court should be reserved for the most serious and exceptional cases, which truly merit the description 'grave crimes' (*R (On the application of B) v Norfolk Youth Court* [2013] EWHC 1459 (Admin)). However, in *BH (A Child) v Llandudno Youth Court* [2014] EWHC 1833 (Admin) it was held that if there was no real prospect that the Crown Court would impose a custodial sentence then the proper venue for trial was the youth court. So even if it is a grave offence if no custodial sentence is foreseen then it should still be tried in the youth court: this is where previous convictions and good character will be factors, but not defining features of the decision; answers A and D are therefore incorrect.

Evidence and Procedure, para. 2.1.6.5

Answer 1.5

Answer **B** — A youth court is a special type of magistrates' court and hears any charge against a child or young person (s. 45 of the Children and Young Persons Act 1933). A 'child' is aged 10 and under 14 and a 'young person' is aged 14 and under 18.

A youth court is presided over by either a district judge or a bench of two or three lay magistrates who receive specialist training on dealing with young people; answer D is therefore incorrect.

Unless there are unforeseen circumstances, the bench must include both a man and a woman (r. 10(1) of the Youth Courts (Constitution of Committees and Right to Preside) Rules 2007 (SI 2007/1611)). Where no man or woman is available—a decision to proceed with the case must be made in open court after hearing submissions from all the parties (*R v Birmingham Youth Court, ex parte F (A Minor)* [2000] Crim LR 588); answers A and C are therefore incorrect.

Evidence and Procedure, para. 2.1.9

Answer 1.6

Answer **D** — The system of courts in England and Wales is a hierarchy, the various courts being related to one another as superior and inferior. An inferior court is generally bound by the decision and directions of a superior court. For example, judges of the Divisional Court and Crown Courts are bound by the decisions of the Court of Appeal. It should be noted that, although the Crown Court is superior to a magistrates' court and enjoys wider powers, it is still a 'lower' court and its decisions are not generally binding on other courts.

When it is said that a decision is binding, or more fully, a binding and authoritative precedent, what is meant is that the principle of law on which the decision was based, or the reason for the decision, is binding. This principle of the law is known as the *ratio decidendi* of the case.

The *ratio decidendi* consists only of the principle(s) of law essential to a decision; answers A and B are therefore incorrect.

A judge, or court as a whole, may sometimes go beyond the facts of a particular case and give an opinion on some connected matter, which is intended to be of guidance in future cases. Such an opinion is known as an *obiter dictum*, and may be persuasive, but not binding, on other courts in a future case; answer C is therefore incorrect.

Such *obiter dicta* are often made where an important point has arisen from the arguments in an appeal case but that point has not been directly raised by either party to the case.

Evidence and Procedure, para. 2.1.4.1

Answer 1.7

Answer **C** — Where a person aged over 18 is charged with an offence that is triable either way, the magistrates' court convenes a mode of trial hearing where the accused is required to indicate a plea of guilty or not guilty. If the plea is guilty, the magistrates may deal with the offence and proceed to sentencing the accused. However, the court may commit the accused to the Crown Court for sentence if it considers the offence is so serious, and/or where the accused's previous convictions are such that it considers its powers of sentencing are inadequate.

Where the defendant indicates a not guilty plea the magistrates will initially determine the mode of trial, by considering the seriousness of the offence, the defendant's previous convictions, and assessing whether their powers of punishment are sufficient (s. 19 of the Magistrates' Courts Act 1980). Answers A, B and D are therefore incorrect.

Evidence and Procedure, para. 2.1.6.4

Answer 1.8

Answer **C** — A magistrates' court may not try a defendant for a summary offence unless the information was laid within six months of the time when the offence was allegedly committed (s. 127(1) of the Magistrates' Courts Act 1980, as qualified by s. 127(2)(a)); this is subject to any enactment which expressly permits a longer period.

In *Atkinson* v *DPP* [2004] EWHC 1457 it was held that, where there is uncertainty as to whether an information has been laid in time, the question should be determined according to the criminal standard of proof and the magistrates should decline to hear the matter unless they are sure that the information was laid in time. The ratio of the decision is that if, on evidence of whatever nature before the court, magistrates doubt the date of the information, such that it could have been laid outside the time limit, they are entitled to, and should, decline jurisdiction. It is a matter of fact for their determination in accordance with the ordinary criminal burden and standard of proof; therefore answers A, B and D are incorrect.

Evidence and Procedure, para. 2.1.7.1

Answer 1.9

Answer **D** — The general principle is that persons under the age of 18 years should be tried and sentenced in the youth court for both summary and indictable offences. They have no ability to elect jury trial. If dealt with by the youth court then sentence also has to be by youth court; answer C is therefore incorrect. The age limit is for the time the crime is committed, not the date of the trail; answer B is therefore incorrect.

However, s. 51A of the Crime and Disorder Act 1998 provides those occasions where a juvenile will be sent directly to the Crown Court for trial. Those occasions are when the juvenile is charged with:

- homicide (murder, manslaughter), or causing or allowing the death of a child or vulnerable adult (s. 5 of the Domestic Violence, Crime and Victims Act 2004);
- an offence under s. 51A of the Firearms Act 1968 applies, that is, the youth is aged 16 or 17 and is charged with an offence contrary to s. 5(1)(a), (ab), (aba), (ac), (ad), (ae), (af), (c) or s. 5(1A)(a) of the 1968 Act, that is, possession or distribution of certain prohibited weapons or ammunition or distributing a firearm disguised as another object;
- an offence that is a grave crime as defined in s. 91 of the Powers of Criminal Courts (Sentencing) Act 2000 where the magistrates decline jurisdiction under s. 24 of the Magistrates' Courts Act 1980;
- a 'specified offence' as defined in s. 224 of the Criminal Justice Act 2003 and where they have been sent for trial as it appears to the magistrates that if they are convicted, the criteria for imposing a sentence of detention for life (s. 226) or an extended sentence (s. 226B) would be met.

So for at least two of the previous reasons he must be sent to Crown Court for trial; answer A is therefore incorrect.

In relation to s. 91 of the Powers of Criminal Courts (Sentencing) Act 2000, the youth court was criticised for retaining jurisdiction in a case involving a charge of rape (*CPS* v *Newcastle-upon-Tyne Youth Court* [2010] EWHC 2773 (Admin)). Similarly, in *FS* v *Wakefield Magistrates Court* [2010] EWHC 3412 (Admin), it was held that attempted rape was a 'grave crime' and the decision to commit the offender to the Crown Court was manifestly reasonable.

Evidence and Procedure, para. 2.1.6.5

Answer 1.10

Answer **B** — The maximum aggregate term of imprisonment which magistrates can impose is six months unless two of the terms are imposed for offences triable either way in which case the maximum aggregate term is 12 months (s. 133 of the Magistrates' Courts Act 1980). Answers A, C and D are therefore incorrect.

Evidence and Procedure, para. 2.1.6.1

Answer 1.11

Answer **D** — The general principle is that persons under the age of 18 years should be tried and sentenced in the youth court for both summary and indictable offences.

Section 51A(2) and (3) of the Crime and Disorder Act 1998 provides five occasions where a juvenile will be sent directly to the Crown Court for trial. These occasions are where a juvenile is charged with:

- homicide (murder, manslaughter), or causing or allowing the death of a child or vulnerable adult (s. 5 of the Domestic Violence, Crime and Victims Act 2004);
- a firearms offence under s. 51A of the Firearms Act 1968, or where s. 29(3) of the Violent Crime Reduction Act 2006 applies (minimum sentences in certain cases of using someone to mind a weapon—note this section only applies to juveniles aged 16 years and over);
- an offence to which the provisions of s. 91 of the Powers of Criminal Courts (Sentencing) Act 2000 apply (offenders under 18 convicted of certain serious offences; powers to detain for specified periods; namely offences carrying a sentence of 14 years' or more imprisonment in the case of an adult aged 21 years and over);
- a 'specified offence' as provided by s. 224 of the Criminal Justice Act 2003 (a specified violent offence or specified sexual offence (dangerous offenders)).

In this case, as it is an offence of allowing a child death he must be tried in Crown Court; answers A, B and C are therefore incorrect.

Evidence and Procedure, para. 2.1.6.5

Answer 1.12

Answer **C** — Criminal trials in England and Wales are either trials on indictment or summary trials.

Trials on indictment take place in the Crown Court presided over by a judge and jury.

Summary trials take place in the magistrates' court before at least two lay magistrates or a single district judge.

Trials for a child or young person generally take place in the youth court that is part of the magistrates' court.

Lay magistrates do not have to be legally qualified and there must be at least two; answers A and B are therefore incorrect.

A district judge sits alone, never with lay magistrates; answer D is therefore incorrect.

Evidence and Procedure, para. 2.1.5

Answer 1.13

Answer **C** — Section 27 of the Courts Act 2003 provides that a justices' clerk may be appointed by the Lord Chancellor only if he/she has a five-year magistrates' court qualification, is a barrister or solicitor who has served for not less than five years as an assistant to a justices' clerk or has previously been a justices' clerk.

The functions of a justices' clerk include giving advice to any or all of the justices of the peace to whom he/she is clerk about matters of law (including procedure and practice) on questions arising in connection with the discharge of their functions (s. 28(4)); answers A, B and D are therefore incorrect.

Evidence and Procedure, para. 2.1.8.2

Answer 1.14

Answer **C** — The youth court has the power to order the juvenile's parent or guardian to attend the proceedings irrespective of who is hearing the case; answer A is therefore incorrect.

If the juvenile is aged under 16 the court must (and if the juvenile is aged 16 or 17, the court may) require such attendance (s. 34A(1) of the 1933 Act). This power equally applies to the attendance of the parent or guardian in the adult magistrates' court and Crown Court.

As JEAVONS is 17 it is a 'may' and not a 'must'; answers B and D are therefore incorrect.

Evidence and Procedure, para. 2.1.9.2

Answer 1.15

Answer **D** — Serving police officers, and staff of the CPS, can serve on juries as this does not offend against principles of fairness where there are no circumstances which would give rise to concerns of bias (*R* v *Abdroikov, Green and Williamson* [2007] UKHL 37). In *R* v *Yemoh* [2009] EWCA Crim 930, the court held that even where a case contained contentious police evidence there was no reason why a police officer should not be a juror; answers A, B and C are therefore incorrect.

Evidence and Procedure, para. 2.1.10.3

Answer 1.16

Answer **A** — Qualification for jury service is provided by s. 1 of the Juries Act 1974, which states:

Subject to the provisions of this Act, every person shall be qualified to serve as a juror in the Crown Court, the High Court and county courts and be liable accordingly to attend for jury service when summoned under this Act if—
(a) he is for the time being registered as a parliamentary or local government elector and aged eighteen or over but under seventy six;
(b) he has been ordinarily resident in the United Kingdom, the Channel Islands or the Isle of Man for any period of at least five years since attaining the age of thirteen;
(c) he is not a mentally disordered person; and
(d) he is not disqualified for jury service.

So, it is five years since attaining the age of 13; answers B, C and D are therefore incorrect.

Evidence and Procedure, para. 2.1.10.3

2 | Instituting Criminal Proceedings

STUDY PREPARATION

This chapter looks at the way in which prosecutions are started. Laying informations and securing the attendance of witnesses, defendants and evidence are basic mechanics of the criminal justice procedure. As with other areas of practical relevance, this means that they will be of interest to trainers and examiners.

QUESTIONS

Question 2.1

The Criminal Justice Act 2003 provides a new method of instituting criminal proceedings where a public prosecutor may issue a document (a 'written charge'), which charges the person with an offence (s. 29(1)). At the same time as issuing a written charge the public prosecutor must also serve on the person concerned a document (a requisition) that requires the person to appear before a magistrates' court to answer the written charge (s. 29(2)).

In relation to this which of the following is correct?

A The written charge must be served on the accused and the court.

B The written charge and requisition must be served on the accused and the court.

C The written charge and requisition must be served on the accused and the written charge on the court.

D The written charge and requisition must be served on the accused and the requisition on the court.

Question 2.2

GOODMAN has had a warrant to distrain property issued against him and is worried about his property and what will happen to it if it is seized.

In relation to this, which of the following is correct?

A Any goods belonging to GOODMAN will be seized and returned on payment of the fines.

B Only certain goods belonging to GOODMAN can be seized and will be returned on payment of the fines.

C Any goods belonging to GOODMAN will be seized and can then be sold.

D Only certain goods belonging to GOODMAN can be seized and can then be sold.

Question 2.3

The procedure in relation to instituting criminal proceedings is provided by the Criminal Justice Act 2003, s. 29, which states a relevant prosecutor may institute criminal proceedings against a person by issuing a document (a 'written charge') which charges the person with an offence.

Which of the following would be a 'relevant' prosecutor?

A The Chief Constable of a police force.

B The Deputy Director legal services of the National Crime Agency.

C The Secretary of State.

D The Crown Prosecution Service only is the relevant prosecutor.

Question 2.4

A company is to be summonsed to court to answer a charge and that company is represented by a firm of solicitors.

In relation to serving this summons, and to comply with the Criminal Procedure Rules 2015, which of the following is correct?

A By leaving it at, or sending it by first class post to, the company's principal office only.

B By leaving it at, or sending it by recorded delivery to, the company's principal office only.

C By leaving it at, or sending it by first class post to, the firm of solicitors amounts to service.

D By leaving it at, or sending it by recorded delivery to, the firm of solicitors amounts to service.

Question 2.5

KEENE had been summonsed to attend court following a private prosecution being taken out against him in relation to an offence that he is alleged to have committed. He has failed to appear and the court is considering whether to issue a warrant to arrest KEENE.

In relation to this, which of the following is correct?

A The warrant can be issued provided the offence is an indictable offence or is punishable with imprisonment.

B The warrant can be issued provided the offence is an indictable offence or is punishable with imprisonment and KEENE has attained the age of 18.

C The warrant can be issued provided the offence is an indictable offence or is punishable with imprisonment and KEENE has attained the age of 18 and there is clear evidence the summons was properly served.

D In these circumstances a warrant for arrest cannot be issued unless the Director of Public Prosecution consents.

Question 2.6

Under certain circumstances a warrant can be issued to arrest a witness and compel them to attend court. The power for this comes from the Magistrates' Courts Act 1980.

In which of the following circumstances can a warrant be issued?

A Where a witness is appearing at magistrates' court only, and only where they have failed to comply with a witness summons.

B Where a witness is appearing at Crown Court only, and only where they have failed to comply with a witness summons.

C Where a witness is appearing at Crown Court only, and only where the judge is certain that it is in the interests of justice to compel the witness to attend.

D In any court where it is in the interests of justice to secure the attendance of a witness and where there is evidence that a summons would not ensure attendance.

Question 2.7

WATKINS is a civilian enforcement officer who is executing a warrant of arrest. The male who is the subject of the warrant demands that WATKINS gives him his name.

Which of the following is correct in relation to the information WATKINS is required to show in relation to executing the warrant?

A WATKINS must provide documentary evidence of his name.

B WATKINS must provide his name, but this can be done verbally.

C WATKINS need only give documentary evidence showing the authority by which he is employed.

D WATKINS need only give documentary evidence showing that he is authorised to execute warrants.

Question 2.8

Constable McCOLL is from a Scottish police force and is on holiday in the south of England. He sees a male from his home town whom he knows is wanted on warrant for several rape offences.

Can he arrest the offender under the warrant?

A Yes, even though Scottish officers generally have no powers of arrest in England.

B Yes, but only as it relates to an offence that is indictable in both Scotland and England.

C No, a warrant issued in Scotland cannot be executed outside Scotland.

D No, however, a local officer could make the arrest properly executing the warrant.

Question 2.9

McGWYER is a civilian enforcement officer employed by the local court and authorised in the prescribed manner. McGWYER is executing a distress warrant at an address when he notices RYAN, for whom he knows an arrest warrant has been issued. McGWYER does not have this warrant in his possession.

Can McGWYER execute the warrant for arrest?

A Yes, a civilian enforcement officer can execute any warrant.

B Yes, an arrest warrant is one that can be executed by a civilian enforcement officer.

C No, a civilian enforcement officer must have possession of an arrest warrant.

D No, a civilian enforcement officer cannot execute an arrest warrant.

Question 2.10

Constable GRAVES, from South Wales Police, carried out a check on the Police National Computer (PNC) on a male. The check showed that a warrant was outstanding against the male, and that it had been issued in the Isle of Man.

Which of the following is correct in relation to the officer executing the warrant?

A The warrant can be executed provided the offence to which it relates corresponds to an offence in England and Wales.

B The warrant can be executed as all warrants issued in the Isle of Man can be executed in England and Wales.

C Warrants from the Isle of Man may be executed in England and Wales where they have been endorsed by a justice of the peace.

D Warrants from the Isle of Man may be executed in England and Wales where they have been endorsed by a district judge.

Question 2.11

Constable PONTING is an officer in an English police force. She has been given a summons, which was issued in Scotland (called a 'citation'). She has been asked to serve the summons on behalf of the police in Glasgow.

In relation to the serving of this summons, which of the following is correct?

A The summons must be served in person by the officer.

B The officer can post the summons, provided it is recorded delivery.

C The officer can post the summons, provided it is sent first class.

D The officer can post the summons to the person's last known or usual place of abode.

Question 2.12

Proceedings may be instigated against a person suspected of a criminal offence.

In relation to these proceedings, which of the following options is available for a public prosecutor under the Criminal Justice Act 2003?

A A public prosecutor must lay information before a justice for a summons to be issued.

B A public prosecutor can issue a 'written charge' charging the person to appear before the magistrates' court.

C The public prosecutor must lay written signed information before a justice for a summons to be issued.

D The public prosecutor must substantiate the information on oath before a justice for a summons to be issued.

Question 2.13

A judge at Crown Court sentences an offender in their absence. The judge issues a warrant to commit the person to prison for a period of 18 months and specifies the place to which they should go. Constable DEAKINS executes the warrant at the offender's home address.

Where should the officer take the offender?

A To the nearest police station, which need not be specified; from there the offender should be taken to Crown Court.

B To the nearest designated police station; from there the offender should be taken to Crown Court.

C To the place specified on the warrant.

D To the nearest prison, even if it is not the one specified on the warrant.

Question 2.14

Detective Constable MATHERS is dealing with a case at magistrates' court where a material witness has refused to attend. The officer also believes that they will not respond to a summons and is considering applying for the district judge to issue a warrant to arrest the witness.

In relation to this which of the following is correct?

A The officer must satisfy the district judge that it is in the interests of justice to secure the attendance of a person who could give material evidence.

B The officer must satisfy the district judge that it is in the interests of justice to secure the attendance of a person who could give material evidence, and that a summons would not procure the attendance of the person.

C The officer must satisfy the district judge by giving evidence on oath that it is in the interests of justice to secure the attendance of a person who could give material evidence.

D The officer must satisfy the district judge by giving evidence on oath that it is in the interests of justice to secure the attendance of a person who could give material evidence, and that a summons would not procure the attendance of the person.

ANSWERS

Answer 2.1

Answer **B** — The procedure in relation to instituting criminal proceedings is provided by the Criminal Justice Act 2003, s. 29 which at section 3 states:

Where a relevant prosecutor issues a written charge and a requisition, the written charge and requisition must be served on the person concerned, and a copy of both must be served on the court named in the requisition.

So both have to be served on the accused and the court, answers A, C and D are therefore incorrect.

Evidence and Procedure, para. 2.2.2

Answer 2.2

Answer **D** — A warrant to distrain property is a warrant which is issued in an effort to collect money. It allows only certain goods to be seized (answers A and C are therefore incorrect) and such goods can be sold (answer B is therefore incorrect) as prescribed by the Criminal Procedure Rules 2015, Part 52.

Evidence and Procedure, para. 2.2.5.5

Answer 2.3

Answer **C** — Section 29(5) of the Criminal Justice Act 2003 defines a 'relevant prosecutor' and includes a police force, the Director of Public Prosecutions (i.e. all Crown Prosecution Service prosecutions), the Director of the Serious Fraud Office, the Director General of the National Crime Agency, the Attorney General, a Secretary of State, or a person so authorised by any of the above.

It extends the definition of 'relevant prosecutor' to beyond just the CPS (answer D is therefore incorrect). It relates to a police force not just the Chief Constable (answer A is therefore incorrect) and it's the Director General of the NCA not Deputy Director legal services; answer B is therefore incorrect.

Evidence and Procedure, para. 2.2.2

Answer 2.4

Answer **C** — The Criminal Procedure Rules 2015 provide that a summons, requisition or witness summons may be served on a person by:

(a) handing it to him/her (r. 4.3(1)(a)); or
(b) leaving it at an address where it is reasonably believed that he/she will receive it, or by sending it to that address by first class post or by the equivalent of first class post (r. 4.4(1) and (2)(a)).

Service of a summons or requisition on a corporation may be undertaken by handing it to a person holding a senior position in that corporation (r. 4.3(1)(b)), or by leaving it at, or sending it by first class post to, its principal office. Where there is no readily identifiable principal office then any place where it carries on its activities or business will suffice (r. 4.4(1) and (2)(b)).

Where an individual or corporation is legally represented in the case, service may be undertaken by handing it to that representative (r. 4.3(1)(c)), or leaving it at, or sending it by first class post to, that representative's address (r. 4.4(2)(c)). As it is first class post and not recorded delivery answer D is incorrect.

It is not only serving the summons on the company that amounts to good service; answers A and B are therefore incorrect.

Evidence and Procedure, para. 2.2.3

Answer 2.5

Answer **D** — Section 1(1)(b) of the Magistrates' Courts Act 1980 provides that, whenever a justice before whom an information is laid has power to issue a summons, they may alternatively issue a warrant for the arrest of the person named in the information, save that:

• the information must be in writing (s. 1(3)); and
• where the person in respect of whom the warrant is to be issued has attained the age of 18, the offence is an indictable offence or is punishable with imprisonment or else the person's address is not sufficiently established for a summons, or a written charge and requisition, to be served on them (s. 1(4)).

An arrest warrant may not be issued in the case of private prosecutions without the consent of the Director of Public Prosecution (s. 1(4A)). This provision was inserted by s. 153 of the Police Reform and Social Responsibility Act 2011; answers A, B and C are therefore incorrect.

Evidence and Procedure, para. 2.2.5.1

Answer 2.6

Answer **D** — The Magistrates' Courts Act 1980 provides that a justice of the peace may issue a warrant where they are satisfied that it is in the interests of justice to secure the attendance of a person who could give material evidence. However, a warrant may only be issued where the justice of the peace is satisfied, by evidence on oath, that a summons would not procure the attendance of the person (s. 97(2)). In addition, a warrant may also be issued where a person fails to attend the court in answer to a summons where there is proof of its service if it appears to the court that there is no just excuse for the failure (s. 97(3)).

Similar powers exist for witness warrants (and summonses) for the High Court and the Crown Court. Answers A, B and C are therefore incorrect.

Evidence and Procedure, para. 2.2.5.2

Answer 2.7

Answer **A** — Rule 13.5 of the Criminal Procedure Rules 2015 states:

(1) A warrant may be executed—
- (a) by any person to whom it is directed; or
- (b) if the warrant was issued by a magistrates' court, by anyone authorised to do so by section 125(b) (warrants), 125A (civilian enforcement officers) or 125B(d) (execution by approved enforcement agency) of the Magistrates' Courts Act 1980.

(2) The person who executes a warrant must—
- (a) explain, in terms the defendant can understand, what the warrant requires, and why;
- (b) show the defendant the warrant, if that person has it; and
- (c) if the defendant asks—
    - (i) arrange for the defendant to see the warrant, if that person does not have it, and
    - (ii) show the defendant any written statement of that person's authority required by section 125A or 125B of the 1980 Act.

All of this must be shown by WATKINS, not just the authority by which he is employed and the fact he is authorised to execute warrants; answers C and D are therefore incorrect. The proof must be documentary and not just provided orally; answer B is therefore incorrect.

Evidence and Procedure, para. 2.2.6

Answer 2.8

Answer **A** — Section 136(2) of the Criminal Justice and Public Order Act 1994 states:

A warrant issued in—
(a) Scotland; or
(b) Northern Ireland,
for the arrest of a person charged with an offence may (without any endorsement) be executed in England and Wales by any constable of any police force of the country of issue or of the country of execution, or by a constable appointed under section 53 of the British Transport Commission Act 1949, as well as by any other persons within the directions of the warrant.

The officer is from the country of origin and can make the arrest, irrespective of it relating to an indictable offence; answers B, C and D are therefore incorrect.

Evidence and Procedure, para. 2.2.6.2

Answer 2.9

Answer **B** — Section 125 of the Magistrates' Courts Act 1980 provides that a warrant issued by a magistrates' court may be executed by any person to whom it is directed or by any constable acting within that constable's police area.

Certain warrants issued by a magistrates' court (arrest, commitment, detention, distress or in connection with the enforcement of a fine or other order), may be executed anywhere in England and Wales by a civilian enforcement officer (s. 125A), or by an approved enforcement agency (s. 125B), and answer D is therefore incorrect. However, this does not extend to all warrants, and answer A is therefore incorrect. An arrest warrant is one of those that can be executed by a civilian enforcement officer, but it does not stipulate that the warrant has to be in the officer's possession, and answer C is therefore incorrect.

Evidence and Procedure, para. 2.2.6

Answer 2.10

Answer **C** — Section 13 of the Indictable Offences Act 1848 provides that warrants from the Isle of Man and the Channel Islands may be executed in England and Wales where they have been endorsed by a justice of the peace; answers A, B and D are therefore incorrect.

Evidence and Procedure, para. 2.2.6.2

Answer 2.11

Answer **C** — Section 39 of the Criminal Law Act 1977 deals with the service of summons etc. in Scotland and Northern Ireland. The Scottish term for 'summons' is 'citation'. A 'summons, written charge and requisition' is said to be 'served' in England and Wales, and a 'citation' is said to be 'effected' in Scotland. Postal service of a summons, written charge, requisition and a single justice procedure notice issued in England and Wales is permitted throughout Great Britain, and a Scottish citation may be serviced by post in England and Wales; answer A is therefore incorrect.

This means that it must comply with posting rules in England and Wales. The Criminal Procedure Rules 2015 provide that a summons or requisition may be served on a person by:

(a) handing it to him or her (r. 4.3(1)(a)); or
(b) leaving it at an address where it is reasonably believed that he/she will receive it (r. 4.4(2)(a)); or
(c) sending it to that address by first class post or by the equivalent of first class post (r. 4.4(1)).

So this means first class post to an address where it is reasonably believed the person will receive it; answers B and D are therefore incorrect.

Evidence and Procedure, para. 2.2.4

Answer 2.12

Answer **B** — Section 29 of the Criminal Justice Act 2003 changes the way proceedings can be instituted in the magistrates' court. The section removes the power to lay an information for the purpose of obtaining the issue of a summons under s. 1 of the Magistrates' Courts Act 1980 (note, this does not apply to warrants), therefore answers A, C and D are incorrect. The purpose of this is to reduce the work of the magistrates' court, and it allows the 'public prosecutor' (which includes a police force in its definition) a new method of instituting proceedings.

Section 29 states:

(1) A relevant prosecutor may institute criminal proceedings against a person by issuing a document (a written charge) which charges the person with an offence.

(2) Where a relevant prosecutor issues a written charge, it must at the same time issue—
- (a) a requisition, or
- (b) a single justice procedure notice.

Evidence and Procedure, para. 2.2.2

Answer 2.13

Answer **C** — A warrant to commit to prison is a warrant of arrest directing that the person be taken to a specified place.

On arrest the constable should take the person to the place specified and obtain a receipt. This is one of the very rare occasions where a person need not be taken to a police station after arrest; answers A, B and D are therefore incorrect.

Evidence and Procedure, para. 2.2.5.4

Answer 2.14

Answer **D** — The Magistrates' Courts Act 1980 provides that a justice of the peace may issue a warrant where they are satisfied that it is in the interests of justice to secure the attendance of a person who could give material evidence. However, a warrant may only be issued where the justice of the peace is satisfied, by evidence on oath, that a summons would not procure the attendance of the person (s. 97(2)). In addition, a warrant may also be issued where a person fails to attend the court in answer to a summons where there is proof of its service, if it appears to the court that there is no just excuse for the failure (s. 97(3)).

Similar powers exist for witness warrants (and summonses) for the High Court and the Crown Court.

The person issuing the warrant must be satisfied of both parts, and the evidence must be on oath; answers A, B and C are therefore incorrect.

Evidence and Procedure, para. 2.2.5.2

3 | Bail

STUDY PREPARATION

In terms of constitutional powers, the granting—and more importantly the denial—of bail is an area of fundamental importance. While there are lots of areas where tenuous human rights arguments have been raised since the 1998 Act was introduced, this one is for real. This area raises lots of questions about an individual's human rights—and therefore potentially lots of questions in exam papers.

For sergeants and inspectors, it is vital to know the extent of powers that exist to restrict or deny a person's bail. Practically this area is sometimes misunderstood, with many police officers (and lawyers) confusing the areas which will permit the police and courts to restrict a person's bail or to deny it altogether.

QUESTIONS

Question 3.1

Officers have arrested ELLIOT for an offence of theft and place him before the custody officer. The custody officer decides that, although further inquiries are necessary, there is currently insufficient evidence to charge and that there are no grounds to detain ELLIOT.

In relation to releasing ELLIOT, what can the custody officer do?

A She can release ELLIOT on bail, which must be unconditional.

B She can release ELLIOT on bail, which can have conditions.

C She can release ELLIOT on bail, which can have conditions and these cannot be varied later.

D As there are no grounds for detention she must release ELLIOT and cannot apply bail.

Question 3.2

There are seven defendants in custody for a complicated fraud inquiry. They have all been interviewed by officers and the senior investigating officer wishes to release the defendants on police bail pending further extensive inquiries. It is anticipated that some of the defendants may be on bail for several months.

In relation to this which of the following is correct?

A There is no time limit for which pre-charge police bail may be granted under the Police and Criminal Evidence Act 1984.

B Although there is no time limit for which pre-charge police bail may be granted under the Police and Criminal Evidence Act 1984, the courts can intervene in exceptional circumstances.

C There is a time limit of six months in which pre-charge police bail may be granted under the Police and Criminal Evidence Act 1984.

D There is a time limit of 12 months in which pre-charge police bail may be granted under the Police and Criminal Evidence Act 1984.

Question 3.3

GERTREND is a French national now living in the UK and has been arrested for manslaughter and is about to be charged with that offence. The custody officer is made aware that GERTREND was convicted in France of an offence similar to manslaughter 11 years ago and sentenced to three years' imprisonment. GERTREND has no convictions at all in the UK.

How will this information affect bail (there are no exceptional circumstances)?

A GERTREND cannot be given bail in any circumstances, as he has a previous conviction for manslaughter from another EU Member State.

B GERTREND cannot be given bail in any circumstances, as he has a previous conviction for manslaughter from another EU Member State and was imprisoned for it.

C GERTREND should be granted bail as he has no convictions at all in the UK.

D GERTREND should be granted bail as power to deny bail to those convicted of similar offences in other EU Member States is only granted to the courts.

Question 3.4

The custody officer is considering whether DENNY, having been charged with an offence of burglary, should be granted bail. The investigating officer believes that bail should be refused, as she suspects that DENNY will commit further offences. The investigating officer believes this because DENNY has previously offended while on bail.

Is the previous offending on bail relevant to the custody officer's decision?

A No, any reasonable grounds for refusing bail cannot be gained from previous incidents.

B No, 'commission of further offences' relates to non-imprisonable offences only.

C Yes, provided those offences committed on bail were burglary offences.

D Yes, provided it is considered with other factors, e.g. the strength of the evidence.

Question 3.5

REED is on bail from the police station for an offence with conditions attached. He has made an application to the police to have those conditions varied but one day later he has not heard whether the conditions have been varied.

What options, if any, are open to REED now?

A REED may apply to a magistrates' court to have the conditions varied as the police have not answered him within 24 hours of the request.

B REED may apply to a magistrates' court to have the conditions varied as the police did not respond to his request immediately.

C REED has no options; as the conditions were imposed by the police only they can vary the conditions.

D REED has no options at the moment as he will have to wait for 48 hours to elapse before he can apply to the magistrates' court for the conditions to be varied.

Question 3.6

MARCATO is in custody charged with rape. The custody officer is deciding whether bail should be granted or refused and they are considering whether bail conditions should be considered. MARCATO has no previous convictions.

In relation to this which of the following is correct?

A The custody officer should only consider conditions where the same objective can be achieved by imposing conditions to the bail, that is, for the person to appear at an appointed place at an appointed time, if this is the case bail *can* be given.

B The custody officer should only consider conditions where the same objective can be achieved by imposing conditions to the bail, that is, for the person to appear at an appointed place at an appointed time, if this is the case bail *must* be given.

C The custody officer cannot consider bail at all as MARCATO is charged with rape.

D The custody officer can consider conditional bail as MARCATO has no previous convictions but the weight should be towards refusing bail.

Question 3.7

GREENING is being bailed by the custody officer and indicates he has had enough of the local police and may well be moving away from the area to live with his brother, who is well known to police in that area. The custody officer asks for that address and if the move is imminent. GREENING replies that it's none of her business.

What is the most appropriate action that the custody officer can now take?

A The custody officer should now refuse bail as she does not know the address of GREENING.

B The custody officer can impose a condition of bail that any change of address must be notified.

C The custody officer can take no action as GREENING has not indicated he is definitely moving address.

D The custody officer can take no action as the brother's address can be easily ascertained.

Question 3.8

FINCH is on police bail for a robbery offence and is due to return next week. Despite a very thorough investigation no eyewitness has been obtained. The investigating officer asks the custody officer to supply to the defendant a notice under s. 47(4) of the Police and Criminal Evidence Act 1984 that their attendance is no longer required. This is done; however, two days later an eyewitness comes forward identifying FINCH as the robber.

Which of the following is correct in relation to action the police may now take?

A The police must serve a notice on FINCH that the bail date has been re-instated.

B The police must attend at his home address and give him a street bail notification.

C The police can re-arrest FINCH and can do so without warrant.

D The police can re-arrest FINCH, but this must be done with a warrant issued by the court.

Question 3.9

MICHAEL (a 13-year-old boy) committed a burglary and stole a car to make good his escape. He was spotted by the police and a short police pursuit ensued (they were unaware that the driver was a juvenile). MICHAEL crashed the car into parked cars and ran off; he was captured nearby by the police. MICHAEL is a prolific offender with many previous convictions. He has been charged with burglary and aggravated vehicle taking. The custody officer is aware that there is no secure local authority accommodation available in the local area.

In relation to detaining MICHAEL at the police station, which of the following is true?

A MICHAEL can be detained as the police are aware that no secure local authority accommodation is available in the local area.

B MICHAEL can be detained as the police are aware that no secure local authority accommodation is available in the local area and there is a risk to the public by placing him in insecure accommodation.

C MICHAEL can be detained provided the custody officer certifies that it would have been impractical to find local authority accommodation.

D MICHAEL can be detained provided the custody officer investigates whether there is secure local authority accommodation available even where there is no such accommodation.

Question 3.10

MURPHY is making a 'live link' bail application at the police station and has attended with his solicitor to make the application to the magistrates' court. The police wish to search MURPHY as they wish to ensure that staff at the station are kept safe.

In relation to this which of the following is correct?

A The police have power to search MURPHY in these circumstances but there is no power of arrest if he refuses; the live link, however, could be cancelled.

B The police have power to search MURPHY in these circumstances and there is a power of arrest if he refuses.

C The police have no power to search MURPHY, however, if he refuses to submit to a voluntary search the live link could be cancelled.

D The police have no power to search MURPHY and as this is a live link bail application they have to facilitate it even if a voluntary search is refused.

Question 3.11

ROWLANDS was on unconditional bail on a charge of assault. The magistrates' court granted bail for a period of four weeks. ROWLANDS failed to appear and a warrant was issued. He was arrested three weeks later and taken before the court.

When he gave evidence relating to a charge of absconding, ROWLANDS stated he had been in hospital at the time of the court date and left hospital a week later. He also stated he had not been given a copy of the court record of the date of his next appearance.

In relation to ROWLANDS' potential offence of absconding, which of the following is true?

A ROWLANDS did not commit the offence as he had reasonable cause not to surrender.

B ROWLANDS did not commit the offence because he did not receive a copy of the court record.

C ROWLANDS still committed the offence even though he had reasonable cause.

D ROWLANDS committed the offence simply by failing to appear in the first place.

Question 3.12

WEBSTER was on bail to attend at magistrates' court at a date in the future. Constable NEWELL received firm evidence that WEBSTER was not going to surrender but was certain to abscond. Constable NEWELL arrested WEBSTER at 11.20 am on Monday, under s. 7(3) of the Bail Act 1976, and detention was authorised at 11.50 am. WEBSTER was taken to court at 10 am on Tuesday and appeared before a justice of the peace at 12 noon. The justice is of the opinion that WEBSTER will fail to surrender in the future.

In relation to what the justice may do next, which of the following is true?

A He may remand WEBSTER in custody as he was brought to court within 24 hours of detention being authorised.

B He may remand WEBSTER in custody as he was brought to court within 24 hours of the time he was arrested.

C He may not remand WEBSTER in custody as he was not put before a justice within 24 hours of detention being authorised.

D He may not remand WEBSTER in custody as he was not put before a justice within 24 hours of the time he was arrested.

Question 3.13

SIMPSON was required to surrender her passport and not to leave the country as part of her bail conditions set by the Crown Court. She was to attend at the court that afternoon and surrender her passport; however, she failed to do so and travelled that evening to Spain. On the day of her trial SIMPSON returned and appeared in court on time.

In relation to SIMPSON's actions, which of the following is correct?

A SIMPSON has committed an offence of breaching her bail conditions and can be arrested for so doing.

B SIMPSON has committed an offence of breaching her bail conditions and can be dealt with by the Crown Court there and then.

C SIMPSON has committed no offences.

D SIMPSON has committed an offence of contempt of court by not complying with her bail conditions.

Question 3.14

MORGAN is about to be charged with a string of serious offences and the custody officer is considering imposing a surety on MORGAN as part of granting her conditional bail.

In relation to this surety, which of the following is correct?

A The surety can be imposed to ensure she surrenders to custody only.

B The surety can be imposed to ensure she surrenders to custody only and can be stood by MORGAN.

C The surety can be imposed to ensure no further offending and surrender to custody.

D The surety can be imposed to ensure no further offending and surrender to custody; it can be stood by MORGAN.

Question 3.15

DEWTRY has been given street bail to attend at his local police station (which is not designated) to be interviewed in relation to a common assault.

Which of the following is true?

A DEWTRY should not have been street bailed to a non-designated police station.

B DEWTRY must be released within six hours of his arrival at the police station.

C DEWTRY must be released or taken to a designated police station within six hours of his arrival at the police station.

D DEWTRY must be released or taken to a designated police station within six hours of his first contact with a police officer at the police station.

Question 3.16

Constable GREIG granted street bail to HENTY and set conditions of bail. HENTY believes that these conditions are unreasonable and wishes to have them varied. He is due at Central Police Station (a designated station) on bail next week.

In relation to varying bail conditions in these circumstances, which of the following is correct?

A HENTY has to attend court to have 'street' bail conditions overturned, they cannot be varied.

B HENTY should attend at Central Police Station and request the custody officer to vary the conditions.

C HENTY should attend at Central Police Station and ask the officer in the case to vary the conditions.

D HENTY should attend at any police station and ask any officer, other than the officer in the case, to vary the conditions.

Question 3.17

KEEN has stood surety for her son at court when he appeared charged with a serious fraud offence. The value of the surety is £100,000. KEEN, however, is concerned her son may not attend at court and wishes to be relieved of her obligation as surety and telephones the officer in the case to ask for that.

In relation to this which of the following is correct?

A KEEN can only be relieved of her duties as surety by a court and needs to apply to the magistrates' court.

B KEEN can only be relieved of her duties as surety by a court and needs to apply to the court her son is next due to appear at, be that magistrates' court or Crown Court.

C KEEN will be relieved of her duties as surety following the phone call but no power of arrests exists until the notification is received in writing.

D KEEN will only be relieved of her duties as surety when she has notified the officer in writing that the accused is unlikely to surrender to custody.

Question 3.18

GREENING is in prison for a six-month sentence and is being considered for the Home Detention Curfew scheme.

In relation to this, how much of the sentence, if any, will this apply to and what curfew restrictions will apply?

A This scheme only applies to sentences of over six months and cannot be applied in this case.

B The last 60 days of their custodial sentence and curfew 10 pm to 6 am.

C The last 60 days of their custodial sentence and curfew 7 pm to 7 am.

D The last 90 days of their custodial sentence and curfew 10 pm to 6 am.

Question 3.19

HENDRICKS has been released from prison and is subject to a home-detention curfew. He is arrested for an offence of theft and is taken before the local custody officer.

What action should the custody officer now take?

A Inform HM Prison Service Parole Unit and ask them to attend and collect the prisoner.

B Inform HM Prison Service Parole Unit and seek their directions on HENDRICKS' disposal.

C Inform HM Prison Service Parole Unit and deal with the prisoner as normal, but he is not entitled to bail.

D Inform HM Prison Service Parole Unit and deal with the prisoner as normal.

Question 3.20

DEWBURY is on a home-detention curfew, and is seen by Constable WYATT in the early hours in breach of his curfew.

What action should Constable WYATT take?

A Arrest DEWBURY and take him to the nearest HM Prison.

B Arrest DEWBURY and take him to the custody officer.

C Follow local policy as there is no power to arrest DEWBURY.

D Request HM Prison Service Parole Unit to revoke DEWBURY's licence. There is no power of arrest.

ANSWERS

Answer 3.1

Answer **B** — The meaning of 'bail in criminal proceedings' is contained in s. 1 of the Bail Act 1976 which states:

(1) In this Act 'bail in criminal proceedings' means—
    (a) bail grantable in or in connection with proceedings for an offence to a person who is accused or convicted of the offence, or
    (b) bail grantable in connection with an offence to a person who is under arrest for the offence or for whose arrest for the offence a warrant (endorsed for bail) is being issued, or
    (c) bail grantable in connection with extradition proceedings in respect of an offence.

This is further endorsed by s. 1(6) which states:

Bail in criminal proceedings shall be granted (and in particular shall be granted unconditionally or conditionally) in accordance with this Act.

As the person, although not charged, has clearly been released 'in criminal proceedings', bail can be granted and answer D is therefore incorrect. Bail can be granted conditionally, because s. 47(1A) of the Police and Criminal Evidence Act 1984 has been amended by the Police and Justice Act 2006 to include conditional bail prior to charge, and these conditions may be varied at a later time; answers A and C are therefore incorrect.

Evidence and Procedure, para. 2.3.1

Answer 3.2

Answer **B** — The Police and Criminal Evidence Act 1984 allows the police to grant bail prior to any charge and this is generally known as police bail. There is NO time limit (answers C and D are therefore incorrect) for which bail may be granted under the 1984 Act and the courts will only intervene where there are exceptional circumstances (answer A is therefore incorrect) (*R (On the application of C)* v *Chief Constable of A* [2006] EWHC 2352 (Admin)). In *Fitzpatrick and Others* v *Commissioner of Police of the Metropolis* [2012] EWHC 12 (QB) police bail was granted on 12 September 2007 and the suspects remained on bail and subject to investigation until it was confirmed that no action would be taken against them in June 2009. The court held that there had been no breach of Article 8 of the European Convention on Human

Rights (the right to respect for private and family life) due to the complex nature of the case.

Evidence and Procedure, para. 2.3.3

Answer 3.3

Answer **B** — Section 25 of the Criminal Justice and Public Order Act 1994 provides for those occasions when bail may only be granted in exceptional circumstances where a person is charged with certain specified offences.

> (1) A person who in any proceedings has been charged with or convicted of an offence to which this section applies in circumstances to which it applies shall be granted bail in those proceedings only if the court or, as the case may be, the constable [answer D is therefore incorrect] considering the grant of bail is satisfied that there are exceptional circumstances which justify it.
> (2) This section applies, subject to subsection (3) below, to the following offences, that is to say—
>   (a) murder;
>   (b) attempted murder;
>   (c) manslaughter...

Subsection (3) goes on to say that if the conviction is for manslaughter there must have been an imprisonment or detention order with that conviction. However subs. (3) has been amended so that previous convictions in other EU Member States are to be treated as being relevant previous convictions if the corresponding offences in the UK would be so treated (Coroners and Justice Act 2009 (Commencement No 5) Order 2010 (SI 2010/1858)); answer C is therefore incorrect. This includes the prerequisite of the original subs. (3) that there should have been imprisonment/detention; answer A is therefore incorrect.

Evidence and Procedure, para. 2.3.5

Answer 3.4

Answer **D** — Section 38(1) of the Police and Criminal Evidence Act 1984 provides that a custody officer need not grant bail if there are reasonable grounds for believing that bail should be refused to prevent the accused, among other things, committing other offence(s). The custody officer should give due weight to whether the accused had committed offences when previously on bail (therefore answer A is incorrect) and also other factors. These factors are:

(a) the nature and seriousness of the offence or default (and the probable method of dealing with the defendant for it),

(b) the character, antecedents, associations and community ties of the defendant,

(c) the defendant's record as respects the fulfilment of his obligations under previous grants of bail in criminal proceedings,

(d) except in the case of a defendant whose case is adjourned for inquiries or a report, the strength of the evidence of his having committed the offence or having defaulted,

(e) as well as any others which appear to be relevant.

Although there are grounds for refusing bail that relate to non-imprisonable offences only, the one relating to 'commission of further offences' relates to imprisonable offences only (i.e. burglary), and therefore answer B is incorrect. The previous offending is not specific to the offence currently charged, and would therefore relate to any offence, and therefore answer C is incorrect—it is information which should be taken as a factor by the custody officer.

Evidence and Procedure, para. 2.3.6

Answer 3.5

Answer **D** — Section 30CB(1) of the Police and Criminal Evidence Act 1984 states:

Where a person released on bail under s. 30A(1) is on bail subject to conditions, a magistrates' court may, on an application by or on behalf of the person, vary the conditions if:

(a) the conditions have been varied under s. 30CA(1) since being imposed under s. 30A(3B),

(b) a request for variation under s. 30CA(1) of the conditions has been made and refused, or

(c) a request for variation under s. 30CA(1) of the conditions has been made and the period of 48 hours beginning with the day when the request was made has expired without the request having been withdrawn or the conditions having been varied in response to the request.

REED will have to wait until the end of the 48-hour period prior to applying to the magistrates' court to have his conditions varied depending on him not withdrawing the request or the police varying them within this time period. Answers A, B and C are therefore incorrect.

Evidence and Procedure, para. 2.3.2.6

Answer 3.6

Answer **B** — Section 25 of the Criminal Justice and Public Order Act 1994 provides that bail may not be granted where a person is charged with murder, attempted murder, manslaughter, rape or attempted rape if he/she has been convicted of any of these offences unless there are exceptional circumstances. As MARCATO has not been convicted of a rape offence answer C is incorrect.

A detained person should be informed of the bail decision as soon as it is made. This can be delayed if the conditions set out in PACE Code C, para. 1.8 apply, in which case the detainee should be informed as soon as practicable.

In reaching a decision as to whether a person should be refused bail the custody officer should consider whether the same objective can be achieved by imposing conditions to the bail, that is, for the person to appear at an appointed place at an appointed time. If conditions attached to a person's bail are likely to achieve the same objective as keeping the person in detention, bail must be given; answers A and D are therefore incorrect.

Evidence and Procedure, para. 2.3.5

Answer 3.7

Answer **B** — Under s. 3A of the Bail Act 1976, conditions can be imposed where it is necessary to do so for the purpose of preventing a person from:

- failing to surrender to custody; or
- committing an offence while on bail; or
- interfering with witnesses or otherwise obstructing the course of justice, whether in relation to himself or any other person.

One or more of the following conditions can be imposed:

- the accused is to live and sleep at a specified address;
- the accused is to notify any changes of address;
- the accused is to report periodically (daily, weekly or at other intervals) to their local police station;
- the accused is restricted from entering a certain area or building or to go within a specified distance of a specified address;
- the accused is not to contact (whether directly or indirectly) the victim of the alleged offence and/or any other probable prosecution witness;
- the accused is to surrender their passport and/or identity card;
- the accused's movements are restricted by an imposed curfew between set times (i.e. when it is thought the accused might commit offences or come into contact with witnesses);
- the accused is required to provide a surety or security.

It is incorrect to state that there is no action the custody officer can take. Where they feel that it is necessary to ensure surrender to custody they may impose a condition of bail that any change of address must be notified; answers C and D are therefore incorrect. The grounds for refusing bail are that the person's name and address cannot be ascertained or that which is given is doubted. This is not the case here as they know who GREENING is and have an address, they even have an indication where GREENING intends to go (although no actual definitive intent was given). The brother is known so his address can be ascertained; it would not be the most appropriate action to deny bail in these circumstances; answer A is therefore incorrect.

Evidence and Procedure, paras 2.3.7.1, 2.3.7.2

Answer 3.8

Answer **C** — The Police and Criminal Evidence Act 1984 provides that a person may be released on bail with a duty to surrender at a given time and date while inquiries are ongoing.

A custody officer, having granted bail to a person subject to a duty to appear at a police station, may give notice in writing to that person that their attendance at the police station is not required (s. 47(4)).

However, nothing in the Bail Act prevents the re-arrest without warrant (answer D is therefore incorrect) of a person released on bail subject to a duty to attend at a police station if new evidence justifying a further arrest has come to light since their release (s. 47(2)).

Answers A and B both have 'must do' but as stated there is nothing preventing re-arrest; they are both incorrect.

Evidence and Procedure, para. 2.3.3

Answer 3.9

Answer **D** — The Children (Secure Accommodation) Regulations 1991 (SI 1991/1505 as amended by SI 2012/3134) provide that a child who is detained by the police under s. 38(6) of the Police and Criminal Evidence Act 1984, and who is aged 12 or over but under the age of 17, must be moved to local authority accommodation unless the custody officer certifies it is impracticable for him to do so, or that no secure accommodation is available and local authority accommodation would be inadequate to protect the child or public from serious harm. Where no secure accommodation is available and the serious harm criterion is met, the child can be kept in police detention. But it is not enough to just use knowledge that there is no secure accommodation to fulfil the responsibility to find some. In *R (On the application of BG)* v *West Midlands Constabulary* [2014] EWHC 4374 (Admin) it was held that the police were fulfilling their responsibilities by investigating whether secure local authority accommodation was available even where there was no such accommodation available. In every case, the police must make enquiries about secure accommodation before authorising police detention; answers A, B and C are therefore incorrect.

Evidence and Procedure, para. 2.3.8

Answer 3.10

Answer **B** — The Police and Criminal Evidence Act 1984, s. 54B states:

(1) A constable may search at any time—
    (a) any person who is at a police station to answer to live link bail; and
    (b) any article in the possession of such a person.
(2) If the constable reasonably believes a thing in the possession of the person ought to be seized on any of the grounds mentioned in subsection (3), the constable may seize and retain it or cause it to be seized and retained.
(3) The grounds are that the thing—
    (a) may jeopardise the maintenance of order in the police station;
    (b) may put the safety of any person in the police station at risk; or
    (c) may be evidence of, or in relation to, an offence...

Answers C and D are therefore incorrect.

Section 46A(1ZB) provides a constable with a power of arrest for defendants who attend the police station to answer live link bail but refuse to be searched under s. 54B; answer A is therefore incorrect.

Evidence and Procedure, para. 2.3.9.1

Answer 3.11

Answer **C** — Section 6 of the Bail Act 1976 creates the offence of absconding. By s. 6(1), if a person released on bail fails without reasonable cause to surrender to custody, he is guilty of an offence. The burden of showing reasonable cause is on the accused (s. 6(3)). Moreover, a person who had reasonable cause for failing to surrender on the appointed day nevertheless commits an offence if he fails to surrender *as soon after the appointed time as is reasonably practicable* (s. 6(2)). The fact that ROW-LANDS did not surrender to the court until being arrested means that, although he had reasonable cause, he failed to surrender and therefore still commits the offence (answer A is therefore incorrect). The offence is not absolute and is not committed simply by failing to surrender to custody, and therefore answer D is incorrect. Section 6(4) of the 1976 Act states:

> A failure to give a person granted bail in criminal proceedings a copy of the record of the decision shall not constitute a reasonable cause for that person's failure to surrender to custody.

Therefore answer B is incorrect.

Evidence and Procedure, para. 2.3.12

Answer 3.12

Answer **D** — Section 7(3) of the Bail Act 1976 states:

> A person who has been released on bail in criminal proceedings and is under a duty to surrender into the custody of a court may be arrested without warrant by a constable—
> (a) if the constable has reasonable grounds for believing that that person is not likely to surrender to custody...

Following arrest under s. 7(3), the person arrested must be brought before a magistrate as soon as practicable, and in any event within 24 hours (s. 7(4)). Note that the section clearly states that the person must be brought before a magistrate (justice) and not brought merely to the court precincts, and therefore answers A and B are incorrect. This requirement is absolute and requires that a detainee be brought not merely to the court precincts or cells but actually be dealt with by a justice within 24 hours of being arrested (*R (On the application of Culley)* v *Crown Court sitting at Dorchester* [2007] EWHC 109 (Admin)). The 24 hours is calculated from the time of arrest and not the time detention was authorised and therefore answer C is incorrect.

Evidence and Procedure, para. 2.3.11

Answer 3.13

Answer **C** — The Divisional Court has held that the purpose of placing restrictions on an individual's movement under the Bail Act 1976 is to ensure that they attend the trial. If the conduct breaching bail is known about at the time, that bail could be revoked, and s. 7 of the Bail Act 1976 provides a power of arrest without warrant if the constable:

- has reasonable grounds for believing that the person is not likely to surrender to custody;
- has reasonable grounds for believing that the person is likely to break, or reasonable grounds for suspecting that the person has broken, any conditions of bail.

However, s. 7 does not itself create any offence. Answers A and B are therefore incorrect.

In *R* v *Ashley* [2004] 1 WLR 2057, the appellant was accused of contempt of court, arising out of breaches of bail conditions. He had been released on bail subject to conditions that required him to surrender his passport and not to leave the country. He broke both conditions but returned to face trial on the appointed day. Although the defendant had breached bail conditions by leaving the country, he did return for his trial. It followed that the judge did not have power to deal with him by way of contempt of court. Answer D is therefore incorrect.

Evidence and Procedure, para. 2.3.10

Answer 3.14

Answer **A** — Section 8 of the Bail Act 1976 states:

(1) This section applies where a person is granted bail in criminal proceedings on condition that he provides one or more surety or sureties for the purpose of securing that he surrenders to custody...

This section has been tested in the courts and it has been held that there is no power to grant conditional bail with a surety to ensure no further offending; a surety can be sought only for the purpose of securing surrender to custody and not for any other purpose *R (On the application of Shea)* v *Winchester Crown Court* [2013] EWHC 1050 (Admin); answers C and D are therefore incorrect.

A person cannot stand as his/her own surety (s. 3(2) of the 1976 Act); answer B is therefore incorrect.

Evidence and Procedure, para. 2.3.7.4

Answer 3.15

Answer **C** — The Criminal Justice Act 2003 allows an officer to 'street bail' an offender as an alternative to arresting him or her and taking him or her straight to the police station, as was required by s. 30 of PACE prior to being amended by the 2003 Act.

Section 30C(2) states:

If a person is required to attend a police station which is not a designated police station [answer A is therefore incorrect] he must be—
(a) released, or
(b) taken to a designated police station, not more than six hours after his arrival.

Answers B and D are therefore incorrect.

Evidence and Procedure, para. 2.3.2.4

Answer 3.16

Answer **B** — Section 30A(1) of the Police and Criminal Evidence Act 1984 states:

> Where a person released under s. 30A(1) of the Police and Criminal Evidence Act is on bail subject to conditions—
> (a) a relevant officer at the police station at which the person is required to attend, or
> (b) where no notice under s. 30B specifying that police station has been given to the person, a relevant officer at the police station specified under s. 30B(4A)(c),
> may, at the request of the person but subject to subs. (2), vary the conditions.

As the conditions can be varied, answer A is therefore incorrect.

The 'relevant officer' as defined by s. 30CA(3)(c) is a custody officer in relation to a designated police station, or a constable or person designated as a staff custody officer in any other police station. A constable involved in the investigation should not deal with the request unless no other constable or officer is available (s. 30CA (5)); answer C is therefore incorrect. HENTY was given notice of which police station to attend, so cannot attend any police station; answer D is therefore incorrect.

Evidence and Procedure, para. 2.3.2.2

Answer 3.17

Answer **D** — Section 8 of the Bail Act 1976 states:

> (1) This section applies where a person is granted bail in criminal proceedings on condition that he provides one or more surety or sureties for the purpose of securing that he surrenders to custody.
> (2) In considering the suitability for that purpose of a proposed surety, regard may be had (amongst other things) to—
> (a) the surety's financial resources;
> (b) his character and any previous convictions of his; and
> (c) his proximity (whether in point of kinship, place of residence or otherwise) to the person for whom he is to be surety.

The Bail Act 1976 provides that a surety may notify a constable in writing that the accused is unlikely to surrender to custody and for that reason they wish to be relieved of their obligations as surety. This written notification provides a constable with the power to arrest the accused without warrant (s. 7(3)). It is the officer who received the notification not the courts; answers A and B are therefore incorrect. It only applies when it is made in writing not a phone call; answer C is therefore incorrect.

Evidence and Procedure, para. 2.3.7.4

Answer 3.18

Answer **C** — The release of short-term prisoners subject to home curfews is provided by s. 253 of the Criminal Justice Act 2003.

The Home Detention Curfew scheme allows prisoners aged 18 years and over, serving sentences of three months or more but less than four years, to spend up to the last 60 days (answers A and D are therefore incorrect) of their custodial sentence on a home curfew, enforced by electronic monitoring.

The prisoner is required to agree to the curfew conditions. The governor at the relevant prison determines the details of the curfew. This will normally be from 7 pm to 7 am and may be varied; answer B is therefore incorrect.

Evidence and Procedure, para. 2.3.14.2

Answer 3.19

Answer **D** — The guidance provided to police forces in relation to persons who are subject to a home-detention curfew, and subsequently arrested for other offences is as follows.

Where arrested, the custody officer is to notify the monitoring contractor immediately of:

- details of the prisoner;
- details of the offence;
- whether the prisoner is to be bailed or retained in custody;
- whether the prisoner continues to wear the electronic tag;

The custody officer is also to notify the monitoring contractor when the prisoner is released.

Where charged, the custody officer is to:

- immediately inform HM Prison Service Parole Unit;
- inform the contractor if the prisoner is to be returned to prison;
- remove and collect the monitoring unit.

Where a person is charged with an offence while subject to a home-detention curfew, PACE Code C in relation to detention following charge continues to apply. The question of bail is not affected by their curfew breach, and answer C is therefore incorrect. The custody officer is responsible for their treatment and disposal, not the prison service, therefore answers A and B are incorrect. Note, this is an arrest for an offence, and is a separate issue from that of the enforcing of his home-detention curfew.

Evidence and Procedure, para. 2.3.14.4

Answer 3.20

Answer **C** — Any reports of a breach of curfew are to be made to HM Prison Service Parole Unit. This unit may make a decision to revoke or vary the curfew order. The relevant prison governor may also make variations to the order. There is no power to arrest any person solely found breaching his or her curfew, as no actual offence has been committed and local policy should be followed, therefore answers A and B are incorrect. Where the police consider that a prisoner subject to a home-detention curfew represents a serious risk to the public, they may make a request for the curfew order to be revoked. Any such request should be authorised by an officer of the rank of superintendent or above and made to HM Prison Service Parole Unit at the Home Office. So the constable cannot seek revocation of the licence directly herself, and answer D is therefore incorrect.

Evidence and Procedure, paras 2.3.14.4, 2.3.14.5

4 | Court Procedure and Witnesses

STUDY PREPARATION

This is what the whole process is all about. Although, logically, this chapter should appear at the end of the book, it makes practical sense to consider its contents here. The mechanics of getting evidence before a court largely come from statute and, as you would expect, contain a fair amount of detail.

It is important to understand who can give what evidence and under what circumstances; it is also important to know some of the more general restrictions that are placed on witnesses' evidence-in-chief and cross-examination.

QUESTIONS

Question 4.1

RAYNOR is appearing at magistrates' court on a charge of theft. At the end of the prosecution case her solicitor makes an application to the district judge that there is 'no case to answer' as the evidential burden has not been met.

In relation to this which of the following is correct?

A A 'no case to answer' application can only be made at the end of the defence case.

B The district judge should consider the application and if the application is successful must outline why it was successful.

C The district judge should consider the application and if the application is unsuccessful must outline why it was unsuccessful.

D The district judge should consider the application and when pronouncing judgment is under no obligation to give reasons.

Question 4.2

FARRER has been charged with attempted murder and is in pre-trial custody. The statutory custody time limit (CTL) is fast approaching and the Crown Court judge set to sit on the trial is trying to set a trial date. A case she is involved in has significantly overrun and no other judge is available prior to the CTL running out. She extends the CTL until a judge is available 12 days after the original CTL expired.

Was the judge correct to extend the CTL in these circumstances?

A Yes, as no judge was available extending the CTL in these circumstances is acceptable.

B Yes, as the original judge is unavailable due to a trial overrunning in these circumstances it is acceptable.

C No, as the trial even if extended has to commence within seven days of the expiry of the original CTL.

D No, these would not be deemed to be unusual circumstances as required to extend the CTL.

Question 4.3

SUTHERLAND is appearing at magistrates' court charged with common assault. He is not represented by a solicitor but is accompanied by his friend who has a law degree but is not a qualified or registered solicitor.

In relation to what his friend can and cannot do in court, which of the following is correct?

A As the friend has a law degree he may address the court but may not question witnesses.

B As the friend has a law degree he may address the court and may question prosecution witnesses.

C His friend may tell SUTHERLAND what to ask witnesses and how to address the court but may not do so himself.

D His friend can only act as moral support, he may not address the court or question witnesses and may not give SUTHERLAND direct advice on legal matters.

Question 4.4

KHAN, who is 21 years of age, was due to appear in magistrates' court for an offence of theft. While waiting in the foyer outside the courtroom someone accused him of being there as a suicide bomber and a fight ensued. The court security ejected KHAN from the building and refused to let him re-enter even for his trial. When his case was called he did not appear and the magistrates decided to hear the case in his absence as KHAN had, by virtue of his conduct, voluntarily absented himself from the hearing of his case.

Should the trial take place in KHAN's absence?

A Yes, as through his actions he has voluntarily absented himself from the hearing.

B Yes, as his behaviour is likely to disrupt the trial they may proceed in his absence.

C No, KHAN is willing and wanting to attend court, but is being prevented from doing so.

D No, only where it would be in the interest of justice can any trial be held without the accused being present.

Question 4.5

BUTLER is suspected of committing an offence and the police are going to interview his wife as a potential witness. It is likely that BUTLER's wife would not be a compellable witness.

In these circumstances what action should the police take?

A The police should not take a statement as it could not be entered in evidence on its own.

B The police should not take a statement as the witness cannot be compelled to give evidence.

C The police can take a statement but it is best practice not to tell the witness that they are not a compellable witness.

D The police can take a statement but they do not have to tell the witness they are not compellable but ought to say that there is no obligation to give a statement.

Question 4.6

BURGESS and PURDY are security staff working at a secure unit holding asylum seekers. A riot takes place and the two security officers will be witnesses at the forthcoming trial of some of the detainees. Prior to the court hearing, a legal training consultancy was used by the security company to provide training for all staff, and BURGESS and PURDY took part in the training. A case study prepared by the training consultancy, for training purposes, contained similarities with the events of the real riot. The training process included a mock cross-examination.

In respect of this training session which of the following is correct in relation to the forthcoming trial of some of the detainees?

A This is coaching of witnesses; it is prohibited by law.
B This is coaching of witnesses; it is prohibited by the courts.
C This is not coaching of witnesses, as it is part of an ongoing training programme.
D This is not coaching of witnesses, as it was not training on the exact evidence that the witnesses would give.

Question 4.7

JOHNSTONE is 17 years old and a witness to an offence of kidnapping. She is to be called to the Crown Court to give evidence for the prosecution, but JOHNSTONE has been receiving threats from the accused's family who have yet to be dealt with for this intimidation. To avoid the accused's family attending and intimidating the witness, the prosecution seek a special measures direction to have JOHNSTONE's evidence given in private.

Whom, if anyone, can the court exclude under this special measures direction?

A Any person, including the accused, but not his or her legal representatives.
B Any person except the accused and his or her legal representatives.
C The public only; the press would be allowed to stay, as would the accused and his or her legal representatives.
D In this case the special measures direction may not be given as it is not a sexual offence.

Question 4.8

Constable GUNTER and Constable HUNT are witnesses in a case of theft. Both officers made pocket notebook entries regarding the incident, and have refreshed their memory from those notebooks prior to giving evidence. Constable GUNTER is now giving her evidence-in-chief and wishes to consult her pocket notebook.

In relation to refreshing memory, which of the following is true?

A She cannot refer to her pocket notebook as she made the notes in consultation.
B She cannot refer to her pocket notebook as she refreshed her memory prior to giving evidence.
C She can refer to her pocket notebook, but only for exact details, i.e. index numbers.
D She can refer to her pocket notebook, provided she states that it records her recollection of the case.

Question 4.9

KHAN and BRADFIELD are jointly charged with robbery. KHAN goes into the witness box and gives an account of events, but BRADFIELD does not give sworn testimony. Counsel for BRADFIELD asks no questions of KHAN in cross-examination. Counsel for BRADFIELD suggests to the jury in her closing speech that the co-accused and a prosecution witness had committed the offence charged, and not her client.

Which of the following is correct?

A Counsel for BRADFIELD can make this suggestion as it relates to the co-accused.

B Counsel for BRADFIELD can make this suggestion as she is not prosecuting counsel.

C Counsel for BRADFIELD cannot make this suggestion as it was not put to him in cross-examination.

D Counsel for BRADFIELD cannot make this suggestion as her client did not give evidence.

Question 4.10

PERKINS has received a summons for a motoring offence and intends pleading guilty by post. PERKINS has previous motoring convictions within the last three years.

In relation to these previous convictions and pleading guilty by post, which of the following is correct?

A If the court wishes to use the previous convictions they must give the accused notice of that intention, but allow the guilty plea by post.

B If the court wishes to use the previous convictions they must give the accused notice of that intention, and direct the accused attend in person.

C The court can use the previous convictions, without giving the accused notice of that intention, but can only use a certified court record of those convictions.

D The court can use the previous convictions, without giving the accused notice of that intention, and can use a DVLA printout to do so.

Question 4.11

ALBERTS is standing trial at Crown Court for an offence of rape. His defence is based on consent and ALBERTS wishes to cross-examine the victim on her previous sexual behaviour, with the leave of the court.

In relation to this, which of the following statements is correct?

A Neither ALBERTS nor his legal representative can ask questions about the victim's previous sexual behaviour.

B ALBERTS can ask such questions, provided they relate to behaviour at or about the same time as the incident charged.

C ALBERTS' legal representative can ask questions about the victim's previous sexual behaviour.

D ALBERTS' legal representative can ask such questions provided they relate to sexual behaviour at or about the same time as the incident in question.

Question 4.12

McMAHON is standing trial on a charge of violent disorder, which occurred during a large-scale public disorder situation. The prosecution relied heavily on the evidence of several police officers, some of whom gave evidence that they had seen the accused committing the offence. The officers were cross-examined only in relation to the evidence they had given. McMAHON, whilst giving evidence, accused certain police officers of a conspiracy to fabricate the evidence against him. This was the first time the prosecution had been made aware of the defence's intention to raise this as an issue. The prosecutor wishes to recall the officers to rebut the accusation.

At this stage in the trial, having closed their case, will the prosecution be allowed to call evidence?

A Yes, but only if the defence accept that there was a misunderstanding between counsel.

B Yes, as they could not reasonably have anticipated this defence.

C No, because this issue was not raised in cross-examination.

D No, because the prosecution must call the whole of their evidence before closing their case—no exceptions.

Question 4.13

WALLACE is a 14-year-old girl who was sexually assaulted. The defendant in the case is about to be tried in the Crown Court and WALLACE will have to give evidence in court. She states that she is likely to be embarrassed about giving evidence in open court, but she is not afraid to give evidence nor is she refusing to give evidence. The prosecution are seeking a special measures direction for the visually recorded interview the police conducted to be admitted as her evidence-in-chief.

In relation to this application, which of the following is true?

A It *must* be granted as the child is under 17 years of age.

B It may be granted unless the court believes it would not be in the interests of jus-tice to do so.

C It will not be granted as the child is not in fear of giving evidence.

D It will not be granted as the child has not refused to give evidence in open court.

Question 4.14

LAVENDER is appearing at Crown Court charged with stealing a bicycle and is representing himself. The jury are sworn and during the opening of the case by the prosecution LAVENDER states that he wishes to be represented by counsel. The trial takes place and the jury has retired to consider their verdict. LAVENDER decides to change his plea to guilty.

What should the judge direct following this requested change of plea?

A The jury should be dismissed and the judge should record a guilty plea entered.

B The jury should be dismissed and the judge should record a verdict of guilty.

C The jury should be directed by the judge to return a formal verdict of guilty.

D The jury should be allowed to carry on their deliberations; a change of plea is acceptable only up until the jury retire to consider their verdict.

Question 4.15

Police are investigating a number of sexual offences at a residential home where most of the occupants have impaired intellect. Charges have been raised and there are a number of victims and witnesses who have severe learning difficulties. They wish to use an intermediary to assist them in giving evidence.

In relation to the evidence to be given by the residents of the home which of the following is correct?

A An intermediary can be used for all of the witnesses/victims.

B An intermediary can be used provided the witness can actually give intelligible testimony.

C An intermediary cannot be used as the witnesses themselves must give intelligible testimony.

D An intermediary cannot be used, however, electronic devices can be used to assist the witnesses.

Question 4.16

CONVOY is a witness to a theft of petrol committed by her husband, and she is being interviewed by the police who are investigating the theft. They do not tell her that she is not a compellable witness and although she is reluctant she gives a statement.

She is called to court but refuses to give evidence against her husband, and the judge rules she is not compellable. The prosecution seeks to admit the wife's statement under s. 114 of the Criminal Justice Act 2003.

Can her statement be admitted as evidence?

A Yes, as her statement was not obtained fraudulently by the police, she didn't ask if she had to make it.

B Yes as there is no requirement to tell a wife she is not compellable prior to obtaining a statement.

C No, the police are required to tell a witness that they cannot be compelled to give evidence where in law they cannot be so compelled.

D No, as the police are aware that she is reluctant to give a statement they must tell her that she cannot be compelled.

Question 4.17

DYER is appearing at Crown Court on a charge of burglary having originally pleaded not guilty at magistrates' court and electing to be indicted. However, fearing a prison sentence he changes his plea to guilty prior to any evidence being adduced. One matter of concern for DYER is that he was accused of stealing a very expensive set of golf clubs. He admits taking them but states they were a very old and cheap set.

What evidence should the prosecution now call?

A Only the accused's criminal record, he has pleaded guilty.

B Only the accused's antecedents and criminal record, he has pleaded guilty.

C The accused's antecedents and criminal record and where necessary evidence to support their version of the facts.

D Evidence that supports their version of events as a previous not guilty plea was entered.

Question 4.18

GRAINGER is 40 years of age and is accused of criminal damage and due to appear at magistrates' court, however, he has failed to appear. There is no notice given by GRAINGER as to why he is not there.

In relation to this which of the following is correct?

A The court should inquire as to why GRAINGER is not present; if no satisfactory answer is received it should proceed in his absence.

B The court should consider whether it should issue a warrant for GRAINGER's arrest or issue a summons compelling him to attend.

C The court may proceed in his absence unless it appears to the court to be contrary to the interests of justice to do so.

D The court must proceed in his absence unless it appears to the court to be contrary to the interests of justice to do so.

ANSWERS

Answer 4.1

Answer **D** — A 'not guilty' plea in the magistrates' court allows the prosecution to call their evidence. The prosecution will begin proceedings by addressing the court in an opening speech.

If the prosecution have established that there is a case to answer (at the close of the prosecution evidence, the defence may submit that there is no case to answer; answer A is therefore incorrect), the defendant can then call evidence. Very occasionally this may be followed by rebuttal evidence being called by the prosecution which is confined to unexpected matters raised by the defence.

At the end of the evidence for the defence (and the rebuttal evidence, if any), the defence will usually address the court, if they have not already done so, in a closing speech. If the defence consider that the prosecution have not established a case to answer, they may make a submission of 'no case to answer'. There is no clear direction as to what would constitute 'no case to answer' in the magistrates' court, and if the prosecution have provided the necessary minimum amount of evidence on which a reasonable court could convict, the trial should continue. In *Moran* v *DPP* (2002) 166 JP 467 it was held that the justices are not required to give reasons in rejecting a submission of 'no case to answer' and this would apply to whichever way the judgment goes; answers B and C are therefore incorrect.

Evidence and Procedure, para. 2.4.4

Answer 4.2

Answer **D** — Regulations 4 and 5 of the Prosecution of Offences (Custody Time Limits) Regulations 1987 (SI 1987/299) set the maximum period during which the defendant may be in pre-trial custody. These limits can be extended but in very limited circumstances:

- the illness or absence of the accused, a necessary witness, a judge or a magistrate;
- a postponement which is occasioned by the ordering by the court of separate trials in the case of two or more accused or two or more offences; or
- some other good and sufficient cause; and
- that the prosecution has acted with all due diligence and expedition.

A trial overrunning and the unavailability of a judge have been found not to be unusual circumstances (*R (On the application of Raeside) v Luton Crown Court* [2012] EWHC 1064 (Admin)); answers A and B are therefore incorrect.

If the CTL is extended there is no further time limit set; answer C is therefore incorrect.

Evidence and Procedure, para. 2.4.7.3

Answer 4.3

Answer **C** — Summary trials take place in the magistrates' court before at least two lay justices or a single district or deputy district judge (magistrates' courts).

The prosecution and defence may conduct their own case in person or be represented by counsel or solicitor (s. 122(1) of the Magistrates' Courts Act 1980). In the Crown Court the prosecution must appear by legal representative but the accused may still conduct his/her own case. An accused conducting his/her own case may be allowed a friend to accompany him/her as an adviser though such an adviser may not question witnesses or address the court (*McKenzie v McKenzie* [1970] 3 WLR 472), and this is the case even if they have a law degree without appropriate professional accreditation; answers A and B are therefore incorrect.

A *McKenzie* friend can give advice in relation to questioning witnesses and addressing the court, although this is still at the discretion of the court; answer D is therefore incorrect.

Evidence and Procedure, para. 2.4.4

Answer 4.4

Answer **C** — Where an accused fails to appear in the magistrates' court in answer to bail the court may:

- issue a warrant for the accused's arrest under s. 7 of the Bail Act 1976;
- appoint a later time when the accused has to appear in accordance with s. 129(3) of the Magistrates' Courts Act 1980;
- proceed in the accused's absence under s. 11(1) of the Magistrates' Courts Act 1980.

The Criminal Justice and Immigration Act 2008 has made certain amendments to s. 11 of the 1980 Act in relation to magistrates' courts proceeding to trial in the accused's absence. Where an accused is under 18 years of age the court *may* proceed in his or her absence (s. 11(1)(a)), and if the accused has attained the age of 18 the court *must* proceed in his or her absence unless it appears to the court to be contrary to the interests of justice to do so (s. 11(1)(b)); answer D is therefore incorrect.

This matter has been dealt with by the courts in *R (Davies)* v *Solihull Justices* [2008] EWHC 1157 (Admin). After his case had been called on, it was discovered that the accused had been excluded from the court building by the security staff because of disorderly behaviour. The justices ruled that the accused had, by virtue of his conduct, voluntarily absented himself from the hearing of his case, and that he should be tried in his absence. The Court of Appeal disagreed and held that even where the accused had been excluded from the court premises due to his disorderly behaviour, this misbehaviour did not justify excluding him from his own trial; answers A and B are therefore incorrect.

Evidence and Procedure, para. 2.4.6

Answer 4.5

Answer **D** — There is a general rule in English law that 'All people are competent and all competent witnesses are compellable'. However s. 80 of the Police and Criminal Evidence Act 1984 outlines that a spouse or civil partner can only be compelled for certain offences.

Where a spouse is not compellable there is no requirement to tell them that they are not a compellable witness before interviewing them about a crime of which their spouse/civil partner was suspected. A statement obtained in such circumstances could be admitted in evidence even though the spouse/civil partner refused to give evidence provided it did not lead to an injustice (*R* v *L* [2008] EWCA Crim 973); answers A and B are therefore incorrect.

However, the prosecution's hand is likely to be strengthened if it were shown that the witness was told that there was no obligation to make a statement (*R* v *Horsnell* [2012] EWCA Crim 227); answer C is therefore incorrect.

Evidence and Procedure, para. 2.4.8.6

Answer 4.6

Answer **B** — The Criminal Justice Act 2003 provides for the use of documents and transcripts by witnesses to refresh their memory.

Section 139 of the 2003 Act states:

(1) A person giving oral evidence in criminal proceedings about any matter may, at any stage in the course of doing so, refresh his memory of it from a document made or verified by him at an earlier time if—

(a) he states in his oral evidence that the document records his recollection of the matter at that earlier time, and

(b) his recollection of the matter is likely to have been significantly better at that time than it is at the time of his oral evidence.

(2) Where—

(a) a person giving oral evidence in criminal proceedings about any matter has previously given an oral account, of which a sound recording was made, and he states in that evidence that the account represented his recollection of the matter at that time,

(b) his recollection of the matter is likely to have been significantly better at the time of the previous account than it is at the time of his oral evidence, and

(c) a transcript has been made of the sound recording,

he may, at any stage in the course of giving his evidence, refresh his memory of the matter from that transcript.

However, the Court of Appeal made clear that training or coaching witnesses in relation to a forthcoming criminal trial is prohibited (*R v Momodou; R v Limani* [2005] EWCA Crim 177), and the facts of this case mirror this scenario. As it is the courts that prohibit it, not statute, answer A is incorrect. Although training firms do provide this service, those using it would have to be very careful that the training did not so closely resemble the case they were witnesses in to be deemed as coaching; answers C and D are therefore incorrect.

Evidence and Procedure, para. 2.4.11

Answer 4.7

Answer **B** — Section 25(1) of the Youth Justice and Criminal Evidence Act 1999 states that a special measures direction may provide for the exclusion of *any* persons from the court while the witness is giving evidence, and answer C is therefore incorrect. This does not include the exclusion of the accused, legal representatives and any interpreter acting for the witness (s. 25(2)), and answer A is therefore incorrect. This direction may be used only where the proceedings relate to a sexual offence, *or* there are reasonable grounds to believe that the witness has been or will be intimidated by any person other than the accused—answer D is therefore incorrect.

Evidence and Procedure, para. 2.4.10.2

Answer 4.8

Answer **D** — The Criminal Justice Act 2003 provides statutory rules that enable witnesses to refer to a document to refresh their memories. This replaces the many authorities and judicial discretion that existed prior to the 2003 Act being enacted. Section 139 of the 2003 Act states:

(1) A person giving oral evidence in criminal proceedings about any matter may, at any stage in the course of doing so, refresh his memory of it from a document made or verified by him at an earlier time if—
   (a) he states in his oral evidence that the document records his recollection of the matter at that earlier time, and
   (b) his recollection of the matter is likely to have been significantly better at that time than it is at the time of his oral evidence.

So the officer can refer to her notebook, irrespective of any factors under which such notes were made, if she states it is her recollection, and such recollection is likely to be significantly better than it is now whilst giving evidence-in-chief. Answers A, B and C are therefore incorrect. However, the Court of Appeal has made it clear that training or coaching witnesses in relation to a forthcoming criminal trial is prohibited (*R* v *Momodou; R* v *Limani* [2005] EWCA Crim 177).

Evidence and Procedure, para. 2.4.11

Answer 4.9

Answer **C** — A party who fails to cross-examine a witness upon a particular matter in respect of which it is proposed to contradict, tacitly accepts the truth of the witness's evidence-in-chief on that matter; this includes the prosecuting counsel and any counsel for the co-accused, so answer B is therefore incorrect. They will not thereafter be entitled to invite the jury to disbelieve the witness in that regard. It is immaterial whether counsel's own client gave evidence or not, what is important is whether they ask questions of a witness: answer D is therefore incorrect. Answer A is incorrect as the fact that the person is alleged to have committed the offence is of no consequence. The proper course is to challenge the witness while he is in the witness box, or at any rate to make it plain to him at that stage that his evidence is not accepted. In *R* v *Bircham* [1972] Crim LR 430, counsel for the accused was not permitted to suggest to the jury in his closing speech that the co-accused and a prosecution witness had committed the offence charged, where the allegation had not been put to either in cross-examination. In *R* v *Bingham* [1999] 1 WLR 598, it was held that a defendant who goes into a witness box exposes himself to cross-examination by the prosecution or any co-accused. This is true even if no evidence-in-chief is offered, or questions asked by defence counsel.

Evidence and Procedure, para. 2.4.16

Answer 4.10

Answer **D** — The procedure for a defendant to plead guilty by post is provided by the Magistrates' Courts Act 1980 and applies to proceedings for summary offences started by way of summons (or requisition) in the magistrates' court (s. 12(1)), or in the youth court for persons aged 16 or 17 (s. 12(2)). The summons (or requisition) is served on the defendant together with a 'statement of facts' and a prescribed form of explanation. This allows the defendant an opportunity to plead guilty and put forward any mitigation in their absence. The magistrates' designated officer informs the prosecution of any written guilty plea.

Where a guilty plea has been received from the defendant, the 'statement of facts' and any mitigation are read out by the magistrates' clerk in open court.

This section is most commonly used for driving offences and provision is made for a printout from the DVLA to be admissible as evidence of previous convictions for traffic offences without the need to give an accused notice of intention to refer to these previous convictions (s. 13 of the Road Traffic Offenders Act 1988); answers A, B and C are therefore incorrect.

Evidence and Procedure, para. 2.4.2

Answer 4.11

Answer **D** — Section 34 of the Youth Justice and Criminal Evidence Act 1999 states:

> No person charged with a sexual offence may in any criminal proceedings cross-examine in person a witness who is the complainant...

This means that ALBERTS himself cannot cross-examine the victim about any matters, and answer B is therefore incorrect. Should ALBERTS wish the complainant to be cross-examined, he must, or the court may, appoint a legal representative. Even when this is the case, there are restrictions on questions that can be asked of the victim. Section 41(1) states:

> If at a trial a person is charged with a sexual offence, then, except with the leave of the court—
> (a) no evidence may be adduced, and
> (b) no question may be asked in cross-examination, by or on behalf of the accused at the trial, about any sexual behaviour of the complainant.

'On behalf of' would include a legal representative, but there are exceptions, with leave of the court. Section 41(2) of the 1999 Act states:

The court may give leave only in relation to any evidence or question only on an application made by or on behalf of an accused, and may not give such leave unless it is satisfied—...

Section 41(3) states that:

This subsection applies if the evidence or question relates to a relevant issue in the case and either—
(a) that issue is not an issue of consent; or
(b) it is an issue of consent and the sexual behaviour of the complainant to which the evidence or question relates is alleged to have taken place at or about the same time as the event which is the subject matter of the charge against the accused...

So in the facts of the question, consent is in issue and counsel could ask questions, with leave of the court; therefore, answer A is incorrect. The House of Lords have considered the very restrictive phraseology of s. 41(3) of the 1999 Act and a person's right to a fair trial. The overriding theme is that the test of admissibility was whether the evidence, and questioning relating to it, was nevertheless so relevant to the issue of consent that to exclude it would endanger the fairness of the trial under Art. 6 of the European Convention on Human Rights. If that test were satisfied, the evidence should not be excluded (*R* v *A (No. 2)* [2001] UKHL 25, [2001] 3 All ER), but still must be recent; answer C is therefore incorrect.

Evidence and Procedure, paras 2.4.16.1, 2.4.16.3

Answer 4.12

Answer **B** — It is a general rule that all of the evidence on which the prosecution intend to rely should be called before the closure of their case (*R* v *Francis* [1991] 1 All ER 225). There are, however, some exceptions to this general rule, and for that reason answer D is incorrect. The three recognised exceptions are:

- evidence not previously available;
- failure to call evidence by reason of inadvertence or oversight; *and*
- evidence in rebuttal of matters arising *ex improviso* (evidence which becomes relevant in circumstances which the prosecution could not have foreseen at the time when they presented their case).

In the facts outlined in the question, only the third exception arises. The principle of *ex improviso* deals with instances where during the case for the defence issues are raised that the prosecution could not have reasonably anticipated when they presented their case. In such instances the judge can allow the prosecution to call evidence in rebuttal of the defence put forward (*R* v *Pilcher* (1974) 60 Cr App R 1). This is true whether the issue is raised during cross-examination or in evidence-in-chief given by a defence witness, and answer C is therefore incorrect. The judge also has discretion to admit evidence of a formal, technical or uncontentious nature, which, by reason of inadvertence or oversight, has not been adduced by the prosecution before the close of their case. In *R* v *Francis* the prosecution called an identification witness to give evidence that at a group identification he had identified the man standing in position number 20, but failed to call any evidence to prove that the man standing at that position was the appellant. The failure was due to a simple misunderstanding between counsel. The discretion of the judge to admit evidence after the close of the prosecution case is not limited to cases where an issue has arisen *ex improviso*, or where what has been omitted is a mere formality, and *Francis* was one of those rare cases falling outside the two established exceptions. Evidence can be adduced in circumstances where the defence do not accept there was a misunderstanding, and answer A is therefore incorrect.

Evidence and Procedure, para. 2.4.18

Answer 4.13

Answer **B** — Section 27 of the Youth Justice and Criminal Evidence Act 1999 states:

(1) A special measures direction may provide for a video recording of an interview of the witness to be admitted as evidence in chief of the witness.
(2) A special measures direction may, however, not provide for a video recording, or a part of such a recording, to be admitted under this section if the court is of the opinion, having regard to all the circumstances of the case, that in the interests of justice the recording, or that part of it, should not be so admitted.

This section replaces s. 32A of the Criminal Justice Act 1988, and clearly outlines that it is not a matter of course that the court makes this direction, therefore answer A is incorrect. It is a matter for the court to decide in the light of all the available circumstances. As s. 27(2) clearly states, the direction may be given unless the court believes it would not be in the interests of justice to do so. This is the test, and not just fear or refusal to testify; therefore, answers C and D are incorrect.

Evidence and Procedure, para. 2.4.10.2

Answer 4.14

Answer **C** — The judge may allow the accused to change his plea from not guilty to guilty at any stage prior to the jury returning their verdict; answer D is therefore incorrect.

The procedure is that the defence ask for the indictment to be put again; the accused then pleads guilty, and the jury empanelled as a result of the original not guilty plea formally return a verdict. Assuming the change of plea comes after the accused has been put in the charge of a jury, the jury should be directed to return a formal verdict of guilty.

In *R v Heyes* [1951] 1 KB 29, the accused pleaded not guilty to charges of stealing and receiving certain property. During the opening of the prosecution case and after advice from counsel who had at that stage been allotted to him, he changed his plea to guilty of receiving. Consequently, where a jury had heard that a prisoner wishes to withdraw his plea of not guilty and admit his guilt, the proper proceeding is to direct it to return a verdict. The judge should not make any announcement of guilt, but direct the jury to return such a formal verdict; answers A and B are therefore incorrect.

Evidence and Procedure, para. 2.4.5

Answer 4.15

Answer **A** — In considering whether a witness is able to give 'intelligible testimony' s. 55(8) of the Youth Justice and Criminal Evidence Act 1999 defines this as testimony where the witness is able to:

- understand questions put to him/her as a witness; and
- give answers to them which can be understood.

Clearly, there is no inherent reason why a person suffering from a mental condition would not make a reliable witness. In *R v Barratt* [1996] Crim LR 495, a witness was suffering from a psychiatric condition and the court considered that her evidence was as reliable as that of any other witness save for certain aspects affected by her condition.

In *R v Watts* [2010] EWCA Crim 1824, where the complainants in a sexual abuse case were all seriously disabled, the court illustrated a number of ways in which special measures directions, including electronic communication devices and the assistance of intermediaries, can be used to enable seriously disabled witnesses to give intelligible evidence, although it also illustrated the fact that such evidence may be difficult to present and difficult to assess in terms of both content and credibility; answers C and D are therefore incorrect.

The witness need not give intelligible evidence where an intermediary can do that for them; answer B is therefore incorrect; however, it is a matter for the jury to determine how much weight to attach to the testimony.

Evidence and Procedure, para. 2.4.8.9

Answer 4.16

Answer **B** — A wife, husband or civil partner is only compellable to give evidence on behalf of the prosecution against their spouse or partner (unless jointly charged) in certain circumstances. A charge of theft would not be one of those circumstances—so in this scenario the wife would not be a compellable witness. So should the police have told her this? In *R v L* [2008] EWCA Crim 973 the court held that there is no requirement to tell a wife that she was not a compellable witness against her husband before interviewing her about a crime of which her husband was suspected; answers C and D are therefore incorrect. A statement obtained from the wife in such circumstances could be admitted in evidence even though the wife refused to give evidence against her husband, provided it did not lead to an injustice. This is irrespective of whether the wife asks or not; answer A is therefore incorrect.

Evidence and Procedure, para. 2.4.8.6

Answer 4.17

Answer **C** — Trials on indictment take place in the Crown Court, generally before a judge of the High Court, circuit judge or a recorder (see *Evidence and Procedure*, para. 2.2.8).

Where there is a 'guilty plea', which must be entered personally by the accused (*R v Ellis* (1973) 57 Cr App R 571), the only evidence which the prosecution needs to call are details of the accused's antecedents and criminal record (answer A is therefore incorrect). Where it is necessary, where there is disagreement about the precise facts of the offence, the prosecution may be required to call evidence to support their version of the facts, known as Newton hearings (*R v Newton* (1983) 77 Cr App R 13); answer B is therefore incorrect.

Any previous not guilty plea is irrelevant, and certainly is not the precursor to a Newton hearing; answer D is therefore incorrect.

Evidence and Procedure, para. 2.4.5

Answer 4.18

Answer **D** — Where an accused fails to appear in the magistrates' court in answer to bail the court may:

- issue a warrant for the accused's arrest under s. 7 of the Bail Act 1976;
- appoint a later time when the accused has to appear in accordance with s. 129(3) of the Magistrates' Courts Act 1980;
- proceed in the accused's absence under s. 11(1) of the Magistrates' Courts Act 1980.

Where the accused's appearance was by way of summons, the court must be satisfied that the summons was served in the prescribed manner before commencing in the accused's absence (s. 11(2)).

The Criminal Justice and Immigration Act 2008 has made certain amendments to s. 11 of the 1980 Act in relation to magistrates' courts proceeding to trial in the accused's absence. Where an accused is under 18 years of age the court may proceed in his or her absence (s. 11(1)(a) of the 1980 Act), and if the accused has attained the age of 18 the court must proceed in his or her absence unless it appears to the court to be contrary to the interests of justice do so (s. 11(1)(b)); answers B and C are therefore incorrect.

The court is not required to inquire into the reasons for the accused's failure to appear (s. 11(6)); answer A is therefore incorrect, but where it imposes a custodial sentence the accused must be brought before the court before commencing a custodial sentence (s. 11(3A)).

Evidence and Procedure, para. 2.4.6

5 | Youth Justice, Crime and Disorder

STUDY PREPARATION

Of all the areas covered by this subject, this one has probably seen the most changes over recent years. Youth justice is a central focus of the Government's overall crime and disorder strategy, and it is therefore a very important area for study.

The overall aims of the Crime and Disorder Act 1998 should be understood, along with the framework for youth justice that it introduced. Reprimands and warnings are important, as are parenting, child safety and curfew orders.

QUESTIONS

Question 5.1

Youth Offending Teams are a multi-agency approach to the reduction of crime and disorder and are formalised by s. 39 of the Crime and Disorder Act 1998.

Which of the following are mandatory representatives on this team?

A The police, social services and education only; all others are co-opted.

B The police, social services, education and probation only; all others are co-opted.

C The police, social services, education, probation, health and others necessary for consultation.

D The police, social services, education, probation and health; there can be no co-opted members.

Question 5.2

A parenting order is created as a way of making parents accountable for the offending of their children, whilst at the same time, giving them the support necessary to take proper care and control of them aimed at preventing the young person from committing further offences.

In what circumstances can an order be made?

A The child has committed an offence.

B The child has committed an offence involving anti-social behaviour.

C The child has committed an offence or a criminal behaviour order has been granted.

D The child has committed an offence or a criminal behaviour or sexual harm prevention order has been granted.

Question 5.3

SEIVRIGHT, who is a youth, pleaded guilty at youth court to a minor case of criminal damage. The court made a referral order to the youth offending team. A youth offender panel was formed and they are now considering making SEIVRIGHT pay for the cost of repair to the item he damaged.

Can the youth offender panel take this action?

A Yes, and this can be done without SEIVRIGHT's consent.

B Yes, provided SEIVRIGHT agrees to the proposed programme.

C No, a financial reparation cannot be ordered, but unpaid work can be considered.

D No, the only programme that can be considered is that of mediation.

Question 5.4

DAVIES is aged 17 and is under arrest for an offence of theft. He has admitted the offence and the officer in the case feels that a youth caution would be the most appropriate way of dealing with this matter. The person who DAVIES stole from wishes a prosecution and does not wish to see a youth caution given.

In relation to this which of the following is correct?

A A youth caution can be given in these circumstances and need not be given in the presence of an appropriate adult.

B A youth caution can be given but must be given in the presence of an appropriate adult.

C A youth caution cannot be given as DAVIES is not under 17 years of age.

D A youth caution cannot be given as the victim does not consent.

Question 5.5

RICHARD is 9 years of age and has been behaving in a manner that has caused alarm, harassment and distress to his neighbours and a child safety order is being considered.

Who should make the application for such an order and to which court?

A The Youth Offending Team to the youth court.

B The Youth Offending Team to the family court.

C The local authority to the youth court.

D The local authority to the family court.

Question 5.6

A parenting order has been imposed on the parents of a child who has been involved in anti-social behaviour. Part of this order is a programme of counselling.

For how long can this counselling last?

A One month.

B Three months.

C Six months.

D 12 months.

Question 5.7

A parenting order has been imposed by the court on the father of TODD and the responsible officer has given directions in relation to that order. The parent is worried about breaches of the order.

In relation to a potential breach which of the following is correct?

A The parent would commit an offence if they fail to comply with the requirements included in the order.

B The parent would commit an offence if they fail to comply with the requirements included in the order or specified in directions given by the responsible officer.

C The parent would commit an offence if they fail without reasonable excuse to comply with the requirements included in the order.

D The parent would commit an offence if they fail without reasonable excuse to comply with the requirements included in the order or specified in directions given by the responsible officer.

Question 5.8

AUDREY is a particularly unruly 15-year-old, in relation to whom the courts are considering a parenting order. Owing to her misbehaviour at home, AUDREY's uncle and aunt are currently looking after her, but they have no legal guardianship.

Can a parenting order be imposed on AUDREY's uncle and aunt?

A Yes, for the time being, they are caring for AUDREY.

B Yes, provided the court's opinion is that they are caring for AUDREY.

C No, the order can be imposed on the biological parents only.

D No, as they do not have legal guardianship.

Question 5.9

CATHERINE is 16 years old and has been arrested for a theft offence and admitted it; there is sufficient evidence to charge. She has already received two youth cautions, one for theft and one for assault. She has no convictions.

Can CATHERINE receive a youth caution for this latest theft offence?

A Yes, as she has no convictions she can receive another youth caution.

B Yes, there is no statutory restriction on the number of youth cautions that a youth can receive.

C No, a youth may receive only two youth cautions before being charged.

D No, as she has a previous youth caution for a like offence a caution here is not appropriate.

Question 5.10

STEVEN has been subject to a child safety order which he has breached.

Provided it is proved to the satisfaction of the court that a child has failed to comply with any requirement included in the order what further action can the court take?

A The court may discharge the order and make a care order in respect of the child.

B The court may vary the order and also make a care order in respect of the child.

C The court may only vary the order, or consider a parenting order.

D The court may only make a parenting order.

Question 5.11

MOORE is 17 years of age and has been convicted of an offence. The court are considering binding the parents over in the interests of preventing the commission by MOORE of further offences.

In relation to s. 150 of the Powers of Criminal Courts (Sentencing) Act 2000 (binding over of parent or guardian) which of the following is correct?

A It shall be the duty of the court to exercise those powers if it is satisfied, having regard to the circumstances of the case, that their exercise would be desirable in the interests of preventing the commission by him of further offences.

B The court may exercise those powers if it is satisfied, having regard to the circumstances of the case, that their exercise would be desirable in the interests of preventing the commission by him of further offences.

C The court may exercise those powers unless there are compelling circumstances not to do so.

D The court cannot exercise these powers as MOORE is not aged under 16 years.

Question 5.12

AMBROSE, who is aged 6 years, has been responsible for causing alarm, harassment and distress to his neighbours and the magistrates' court is considering a child safety order under s. 11 of the Crime and Disorder Act 1998.

Can a child safety order be issued?

A Yes, on these factors alone a child safety order could be issued.

B Yes, provided he has also committed an offence that had he been aged 10 or over would have constituted an offence.

C No, a child safety order can only be issued to those who have reached at least 10 years of age.

D No, a child safety order can only be issued to those who have reached at least 8 years of age.

Question 5.13

Section 150 of the Powers of Criminal Courts (Sentencing) Act 2000 provides for the binding over of a parent or guardian to order them to enter into a recognizance to take proper care of and exercise proper control over their child following conviction.

For how long can this recognizance be imposed?

A Three months.

B Six months.

C One year.

D Three years.

Question 5.14

The Education Act 1996 provides that penalty notices can be issued to parents or guardians who fail to ensure the regular attendance of their child who is registered at a state school, or fail to ensure that their excluded child is not found in a public place during school hours without a justifiable reason.

Which of the following is correct in relation to children to whom this applies?

A Any child provided they are or have been in full time education.

B A child of compulsory school age (5–16).

C A child of compulsory school age (5–16) or 17 if in sixth form.

D A child of school age (5–15).

Question 5.15

An authority to remove truants to designated premises is in effect and Constable McGIVERN found LAWRENCE, who is of compulsory school age, absent from school with no lawful authority.

What should Constable McGIVERN do?

A LAWRENCE must be returned to his own school.

B LAWRENCE must be returned to any school in the local education authority.

C LAWRENCE can be returned to any place the local authority has nominated.

D LAWRENCE can be returned to any place the local education authority has nominated.

Question 5.16

Constable O'HARA is on foot patrol in the city centre when she comes across a young male who appears to be about 13 years of age. She confirms his age and asks why he is not in school. The young boy states his parents are 'ageing hippies' and they educate him at home on his houseboat.

What should Constable O'HARA do?

A The boy must be returned to his home address.

B The boy must be returned to any school in the local education authority.

C The boy can be returned to any place the local education authority has nominated.

D The boy should be left alone, unless any offences are apparent.

Question 5.17

MULHOLLAND has committed an offence and is in police custody. The officer in the case considers that they would be suitable to receive a youth conditional caution and that this is the most appropriate way of disposing of the case.

In relation to this which of the following is correct?

A The custody officer is responsible for the decision to impose a youth conditional caution having identified a suitable case.

B The custody officer is responsible for the decision to impose a youth conditional caution; the OIC has a responsibility for identifying suitable cases.

C The Crown Prosecutor is responsible for the decision to impose a youth conditional caution; the OIC has a responsibility for identifying suitable cases.

D The Crown Prosecutor is responsible for the decision to impose a youth conditional caution; the custody officer has a responsibility for identifying suitable cases.

Question 5.18

STEPHENS is aged 14 and has committed an offence of criminal damage for which he will receive a youth caution. His parents, however, are not available and an appropriate adult is required.

Which of the following would be an 'appropriate adult' in these circumstances?

A STEPHENS's 17-year-old brother.

B STEPHENS's 21-year-old neighbour.

C A 42-year-old police civilian.

D Any police officer not connected with the case.

Question 5.19

TAYLOR does not attend school regularly and her parents are aware of this and do nothing to ensure she attends. Section 444A of the Education Act 1996 provides a penalty notice scheme for parents or guardians of children failing to attend school regularly.

Who can issue such a penalty notice?

A A police constable only.

B A police constable and authorised teacher only.

C A police constable and authorised teacher or authorised officer of the local authority.

D An authorised officer of the local authority only.

ANSWERS

Answer 5.1

Answer **C** — Youth offending teams are multi-agency teams that are coordinated by a local authority and were introduced with the intention of reducing the risk of young people offending and re-offending, and to provide counsel and rehabilitation to those who do offend.

Section 39(5) of the Crime and Disorder Act 1998 states:

A youth offending team shall include at least one of each of the following, namely—
(a) an officer of a local probation board or an officer of a provider of probation services;
(aa) where the local authority is in England, a person with experience of social work in relation to children nominated by the director of children's services appointed by the local authority under section 18 of the Children Act 2004;
(b) where the local authority is in Wales, a social worker of the local authority social services department;
(c) a police officer;
(d) a person nominated by a Clinical Commissioning Group or a Local Health Board any part of whose area lies within the local authority's area;
(da) where the local authority is in England, a person with experience in education nominated by the director of children's services appointed by the local authority under section 18 of the Children Act 2004;
(e) where the local authority is in Wales, a person nominated by the chief education officer appointed by the local authority under section 532 of the Education Act 1996.

Answers A and B are incorrect as they do not contain all these agencies.

In addition to those included as members of a youth offending team it may also include such other persons as the local authority thinks appropriate after consulting the other bodies involved (s. 39(6)); answer D is therefore incorrect.

Evidence and Procedure, para. 2.5.3

Answer 5.2

Answer **D** — Parenting orders are provided by s. 8 of the Crime and Disorder Act 1998 which states:

(1) This section applies where, in any court proceedings—
(a) a child safety order is made in respect of a child, or the court determines on an application under section 12(6) below that a child has failed to comply with any requirement included in such an order;

(aa) a parental compensation order is made in relation to a child's behaviour;

(b) an injunction is granted under section 1 of the Anti-social Behaviour, Crime and Policing Act 2014, an order is made under section 22 of that Act or a sexual harm prevention order is made in respect of a child or young person;

(c) a child or young person is convicted of an offence...

In relation to subs. (1)(b), the order under s. 22 of the 2014 Act is a criminal behaviour order, and a sexual harm prevention order means an order under s. 103A of the Sexual Offences Act 2003; answers A, B and C are therefore incorrect.

Evidence and Procedure, para. 2.5.5.1

Answer 5.3

Answer **B** — Sections 23 to 27 of the Powers of Criminal Courts (Sentencing) Act 2000 deal with youth offender contracts. This is a programme of behaviour to prevent re-offending, but it has to be agreed between the offender and the panel (s. 23(5)), and therefore answer A is incorrect. The terms of the programme may include a number of provisions; attendance at mediation sessions is one of them, but is by no means exclusive, and answer D is therefore incorrect. The measures may include: financial or other reparation to the victim; attendance at mediation sessions; unpaid work or service; curfew requirements; educational attendance; rehabilitation for drugs or alcohol misuse and therefore answer C is incorrect.

Evidence and Procedure, para. 2.5.3

Answer 5.4

Answer **B** — Section 66ZA of the Crime and Disorder Act 1998 states:

(1) A constable may give a child or young person ('Y') a caution under this section (a 'youth caution') if—

(a) the constable decides that there is sufficient evidence to charge Y with an offence,

(b) Y admits to the constable that Y committed the offence, and

(c) the constable does not consider that Y should be prosecuted or given a youth conditional caution in respect of the offence.

(2) A youth caution must be given in the presence of an appropriate adult.

There is no need to obtain the victim's consent and therefore answer D is incorrect. The youth caution can be given to a 17-year-old but must be done in the presence of an appropriate adult; answers A and C are therefore incorrect.

Evidence and Procedure, para. 2.5.4

Answer 5.5

Answer **D** — Section 11 of the Crime and Disorder Act 1998 states:

> (1) Subject to subsection (2) below, if the family court, on the application of a local authority, is satisfied that one or more of the conditions specified in subsection (3) below are fulfilled with respect to a child under the age of 10, it may make an order (a 'child safety order').

Thus the local authority makes the application to the family court; answers A, B and C are therefore incorrect.

Evidence and Procedure, para. 2.5.6

Answer 5.6

Answer **B** — Parenting orders are defined by s. 8 of the Crime and Disorder Act 1998:

> (4) A parenting order is an order which requires the parent—
>   (a) to comply, for a period not exceeding twelve months, with such requirements as are specified in the order, and
>   (b) subject to subsection (5) below, to attend, for a concurrent period not exceeding three months and not more than once in any week, such counselling or guidance sessions as may be specified in directions given by the responsible officer...

As can be seen, the period is three months; answers A, C and D are therefore incorrect.

Evidence and Procedure, para. 2.5.5.1

Answer 5.7

Answer **D** — Parenting orders are provided by s. 8 of the Crime and Disorder Act 1998 and breaches are dealt with by s. 9 which states:

> If while a parenting order is in force the parent without reasonable excuse fails to comply with any requirement included in the order, or specified in directions given by the responsible officer, he shall be liable on summary conviction to a fine not exceeding level 3 on the standard scale.

So it is both the order and directions, but there is a 'reasonable excuse' clause; answers A, B and C are therefore incorrect.

Evidence and Procedure, para. 2.5.5.2

Answer 5.8

Answer **B** — Under s. 8(2) of the Crime and Disorder Act 1998, a parenting order may be made against:

- one or both biological parents (this could include an order against a father who may not be married to the mother);
- a person who is a guardian.

Therefore, answer C is incorrect.

A guardian is defined as any person who, in the opinion of the court, has for the time being the care of a child or young person (s. 117(1)). It is not a matter of 'legal' guardianship (even if somebody has temporary care and control of a child), as it is the court that will decide who is *in fact* a 'guardian'; therefore, answers A and D are incorrect.

Evidence and Procedure, para. 2.5.5.1

Answer 5.9

Answer **B** — A youth caution is a formal out-of-court disposal intended to provide a proportionate and effective response to offending behaviour and can be used for any offence provided that the statutory criteria are satisfied. There is no statutory restriction on the number of youth cautions that a youth can receive, and a youth may receive a youth caution even if he/she has previous convictions (answer A is therefore incorrect), reprimands, warnings, youth cautions (answers C and D are therefore incorrect) and youth conditional cautions.

Evidence and Procedure, para. 2.5.4

Answer 5.10

Answer **A** — Child safety orders are designed to help prevent children under 10 from turning to crime. Such orders are concerned with the child's potential offending behaviour and in practice are likely to be used in conjunction with parenting orders under s. 8 of the Crime and Disorder Act 1998 but this will not be used where a child safety order is breached; answers C and D are therefore incorrect.

Where it is proved to the satisfaction of the court that a child has failed to comply with any requirement included in the order, it may discharge the order and make in respect of the child a care order; answer B is therefore incorrect.

Evidence and Procedure, para. 2.5.6

Answer 5.11

Answer **B** — Section 150 of the Powers of Criminal Courts (Sentencing) Act 2000 provides for the binding over of a parent or guardian and states:

(1) Where a child or young person (that is to say, any person aged under 18) is convicted of an offence, the powers conferred by this section shall be exercisable by the court by which he is sentenced for that offence, and where the offender is aged under 16 when sentenced it shall be the duty of the court—

(a) to exercise those powers if it is satisfied, having regard to the circumstances of the case, that their exercise would be desirable in the interests of preventing the commission by him of further offences; and

(b) if it does not exercise them, to state in open court that it is not satisfied as mentioned in paragraph (a) above and why it is not so satisfied;

but this subsection has effect subject to section 19(5) above and paragraph 13(5) of Schedule 1 to this Act (cases where referral orders made or extended).

(2) The powers conferred by this section are as follows—

(a) with the consent of the offender's parent or guardian, to order the parent or guardian to enter into a recognizance to take proper care of him and exercise proper control over him; and

(b) if the parent or guardian refuses consent and the court considers the refusal unreasonable, to order the parent or guardian to pay a fine not exceeding £1,000;

and where the court has passed a community sentence on the offender, it may include in the recognizance provision that the offender's parent or guardian ensure that the offender complies with the requirements of that sentence.

As MOORE is 17 these powers still apply; answer D is therefore incorrect. If MOORE were under 16 the court must exercise those powers but between 16 and 18 they are not mandated; answers A and C are therefore incorrect.

Evidence and Procedure, para. 2.5.5.3

Answer 5.12

Answer **A** — Before a child safety order under s. 11 of the Crime and Disorder Act 1998 can be made the court must be satisfied that one or more of the following three conditions, provided by s. 11(3) of the Act, are fulfilled before making an order:

• that the child has committed an act which, if he had been aged 10 or over, would have constituted an offence;

• that the order is necessary for the purpose of preventing the commission by the child of such an act; and

- that the child has acted in a manner that caused or was likely to cause harassment, alarm or distress to one or more persons not of the same household as him/ herself.

As can be seen, although more than one condition may be evident, only one is required; answer B is therefore incorrect.

There is no minimum age for an order; answers C and D are therefore incorrect.

Evidence and Procedure, para. 2.5.6

Answer 5.13

Answer **D** — The recognizance can be imposed on the parent or guardian for up to three years or until the offender is aged 18, whichever is the shorter (s. 150(4) of the Powers of Criminal Courts (Sentencing) Act 2000); answers A, B and C are therefore incorrect.

Evidence and Procedure, para. 2.5.5.3

Answer 5.14

Answer **B** — The Education Act 1996 provides that penalty notices can be issued to parents or guardians who fail to ensure the regular attendance of their child of compulsory school age (5–16) who is registered at a state school, or fail to ensure that their excluded child is not found in a public place during school hours without a justifiable reason; answers A, C and D are therefore incorrect.

Evidence and Procedure, para. 2.5.7.1

Answer 5.15

Answer **C** — A local authority is under an obligation by s. 16 of the Crime and Disorder Act 1998 to designate premises in a police area ('designated premises') as premises to which children and young persons of compulsory school age may be removed under this section, and they must notify the chief officer of police for that area of the designation. When an order to remove truants has been issued, if a constable has reasonable cause to believe that a child or young person found by him in a public place in a specified area during a specified period:

- is of compulsory school age; *and*
- is absent from a school without lawful authority,

the constable may remove the child or young person to designated premises, or to the school from which he is absent. He does not *have* to be returned to either his own school, or another school in the local education authority area, so answers A and B are therefore incorrect. Provided a particular place has been designated (or nominated) by the local authority, the child may be returned there. Note, it is the local authority who designates, not the local education authority; answer D is therefore incorrect.

Evidence and Procedure, para. 2.5.7.1

Answer 5.16

Answer **D** — Section 16 of the Crime and Disorder Act 1998 provides the police powers in relation to dealing with truants:

> (3) If a constable has reasonable cause to believe that a child or young person found by him in a public place in a specified area during a specified period—
> (a) is of compulsory school age; and
> (b) is absent from school without lawful authority,
> the constable may remove the child or young person to designated premises, or to the school from which he is so absent.

The powers apply to those children and young people who are pupils registered at a school. They do not apply to children and young people educated at home who, quite lawfully, are out and about, alone and unaccompanied, during school hours. Therefore there is no power to remove the youth to anywhere; answers A, B and C are therefore incorrect.

Evidence and Procedure, para. 2.5.7.1

Answer 5.17

Answer **D** — Another means of disposal for young persons aged 10 to 17, outside the usual court process, is the youth conditional caution. This is a caution that may be given in respect of an offence and which has conditions attached to it (Crime and Disorder Act 1998, ss. 66A–66H).

The decision to impose such a caution rests with a Crown Prosecutor, and although the police have no powers in respect of these cautions, custody officers have a responsibility for identifying suitable cases.

It is therefore the Crown Prosecutor and custody officer who have responsibilities and not the OIC; answers A, B and C are therefore incorrect.

Evidence and Procedure, para. 2.5.4

Answer 5.18

Answer **B** — Section 66ZA(7) of the Crime and Disorder Act 1998 provides that an 'appropriate adult' means a parent or guardian, a person representing the authority or organisation of a child or young person in care, a social worker of a local authority, or if no person falls within these categories any responsible person aged 18 or over who is not a police officer or a person employed by the police.

As the brother is only 17, and anyone connected with the police cannot perform this function, then answers A, C and D are incorrect and answer B is the only correct option.

Evidence and Procedure, para. 2.5.4

Answer 5.19

Answer **C** — Section 444A of the Education Act 1996 provides a penalty notice scheme for parents or guardians of children failing to attend school regularly. The notices will normally be issued by a designated local authority officer, headteachers (and authorised deputy headteachers and assistant headteachers), police officers and community support officers. So it is all three; answers A, B and D are therefore incorrect.

Evidence and Procedure, para. 2.5.7.1

6 | Exclusion of Admissible Evidence

STUDY PREPARATION

There are few more frustrating experiences for police officers than to have brought a person before the court and presented the evidence against them, only to have some of that evidence excluded.

This area of law has grown up partly through the common law decisions of the higher courts and partly through statute. And now there is the additional force of the Human Rights Act 1998, which has focused attention on the defendant's inalienable right to a fair trial and the attendant safeguards under Art. 6 of the European Convention on Human Rights.

Many of the occasions where admissible evidence is later excluded by the courts arise in suspect interviews, or on other occasions where the police officer(s) concerned say or do something that renders any response by the defendant unreliable or its introduction in evidence unfair. Therefore, areas of confessions and oppression are key features in this chapter, as are the practical consequences of an exclusion ruling being made.

QUESTIONS

Question 6.1

WILLIAMS and THOMPSON were jointly charged with possessing stolen property. In his police interview, WILLIAMS admitted that he knew the goods were stolen but stated that THOMPSON had no knowledge of that.

WILLIAMS pleaded guilty. THOMPSON pleaded not guilty and at his trial argued that he did not know that property amounted to stolen goods. WILLIAMS indicated he would be unwilling to give evidence at court on behalf of THOMPSON and was therefore not called by the defence. Instead, the defence sought to rely on WILLIAMS' statements in his police interview.

Will this previous confession by WILLIAMS be admissible in THOMPSON's trial?

A The statement will be allowed as he is no longer a defendant, he is only a witness.

B The statement will be allowed as a confession made by one accused person can be given in evidence for another person charged in the same proceedings.

C The statement won't be allowed as WILLIAMS is no longer charged in the same proceedings.

D The statement won't be allowed as the confession was from WILLIAMS not from THOMPSON and is therefore inadmissible.

Question 6.2

MARTIN was suspected of an offence and a decision was made to take a hair sample from him for DNA comparison. MARTIN was going bald and asked if the hair could be taken from somewhere other than his head. The officer who was asked to take the sample laughed and grabbed a big handful of hair on the suspect's head and pulled it out. MARTIN was really upset over his treatment, which was clearly a breach of Code D, para. 6.1 (note 6A) of the Police and Criminal Evidence Act 1984 Codes of Practice. The sample gave a positive DNA result which was to form part of the case against MARTIN.

Is this DNA evidence likely to be excluded due to the breach of the codes of practice when it was obtained?

A Yes, there was a clear breach of the codes of practice, and it was more than a trifling, minor breach and will lead to exclusion.

B Yes, any breach of the codes of practice that was deliberate and malevolent will lead to exclusion of the evidence.

C No, the evidence will be admitted on the basis that the means used to obtain it have done nothing to cast doubt on its reliability and strength.

D No, any physical evidence obtained can never be ruled to be unreliable.

Question 6.3

FRENCH is standing trial at the Crown Court, charged with blackmail. The defence ask the judge to exclude certain evidence that the prosecution seek to adduce exercising common law powers retained by s. 82(3) of the Police and Criminal Evidence Act 1984.

For evidence to be excluded at common law the court will do what?

A Concern itself with the effect that the evidence will have at trial, rather than how the evidence was obtained.

B Concern itself with how the evidence was obtained rather than the effect that the evidence will have at trial.

C Concern itself with how the evidence was obtained and in particular have there been any breaches of the Codes of Practice.

D Concern itself with how the evidence was presented during the trial considering what effect that evidence will have on the trial.

Question 6.4

TIMPKINS was arrested for murder. On being told that if he confessed he would be charged with manslaughter only, TIMPKINS stated he had shot the victim in self-defence. TIMPKINS then told the officers where to find the gun, which he had hidden in a hedge. The gun was found, and at a second interview TIMPKINS identified it as the one he had used, again because he believed he would be charged with manslaughter only. Ballistic evidence showed it was the weapon used. TIMPKINS was charged with murder. At TIMPKINS' trial, the judge ruled that the confession obtained at the first interview would be excluded as it was 'unreliable'.

In relation to evidence the police can now give, which of the following statements is true?

A The police can state that TIMPKINS identified the gun, as this was during the second interview, which should be allowed.

B The police can state that they found a gun where TIMPKINS told them to look, and that it was the gun used in the shooting.

C The police may not be able to make a connection between TIMPKINS and the gun.

D The police will be able to state that TIMPKINS said he had used the gun, as this was during the second interview, which should be allowed.

Question 6.5

VENTHAM was suspected by his employers of stealing from work colleagues and was interviewed by the employers. He was told that if he admitted that he had been stealing he would be sacked but that the police would not be contacted. If he denied the thefts the police would be called to investigate. He told his employer that he had stolen and they contacted the police anyway. He was charged with theft and his 'confession' was sought to be adduced in evidence against him.

In relation to this which of the following is correct?

A This confession would not be allowed as it was not made to a person in authority and is therefore inadmissible.

B This confession would not be allowed as it would be deemed to be unreliable due to the inducement to make it.

C This confession would be allowed as the inducement was not made by a person in authority and therefore would be admissible.

D The confession would be allowed provided VENTHAM was asked about it during a formal police interview as a significant statement.

Question 6.6

MORGAN has confessed to the police about a burglary he was suspected of. At his trial it is submitted that the confession was not voluntarily given and that it is therefore unreliable.

In relation to the confession evidence which of the following is correct?

A The prosecution need only satisfy the judge that the confession was made voluntarily.

B The prosecution need only satisfy the judge that the confession was made voluntarily, and if successful there will be no direction to the jury.

C The prosecution must satisfy the judge that the confession was made voluntarily and the judge can advise the jury on the reliability if they choose.

D The prosecution must satisfy the judge that the confession was made voluntarily and the judge must advise the jury on the reliability.

Question 6.7

BLOUNT left explicit graffiti messages in a public lavatory, seeking sex with girls aged between 8 and 13 years, and asking them to follow him on Twitter, leaving his Twitter name. The police became aware and monitored his social media account. With the relevant authority a police officer followed BLOUNT on Twitter and sent several messages implying that she was an 12-year-old girl, and interested in meeting him. BLOUNT replied, arranging a meeting and describing the various sexual acts he would perform on her. At the meeting, he was arrested and later charged with attempting to incite a child under the age of 13 to engage in sexual activity, contrary to s. 8 of the Sexual Offences Act 2003.

In relation to this which of the following is correct with regard to entrapment?

A BLOUNT is guilty as the police provided no more than an opportunity to commit the offence.

B BLOUNT is guilty as soon as he left the messages in the toilet; the police action was no more than an attempt to locate and arrest him.

C BLOUNT is not guilty, as the officer purporting to be the child was not under 13 years of age, the offence could never be committed.

D BLOUNT is not guilty as the police operated using a false persona and therefore this would be entrapment.

Question 6.8

COSTELO wished to arrange a contract killing of her husband. In the two years preceding his death, she repeatedly stated that she wanted him killed and asked various witnesses whether they would help her kill him. She associated with SHERD who was a customer of her sandwich shop. SHERD associated with RYRIE. At the trial the prosecution have evidence that SHERD twice sent to RYRIE large amounts of money contained in sandwich bags from COSTELO's shop.

All three are charged jointly with murder, the main evidence being a confession by RYRIE, made to his girlfriend, that he killed COSTELO's husband and that SHERD was the 'middleman'. There is only other circumstantial evidence against SHERD.

In relation to this confession by RYRIE which of the following is correct?

A The confession is not admissible as it was made to a friend and not to the police.

B The confession is not admissible against the co-defendants as a confession is relevant and admissible only against its maker.

C The jury can only consider the confession in relation to RYRIE's guilt, not whilst considering the co-defendants' guilt.

D The jury are entitled to take RYRIE's confession into account whilst considering the co-defendants' guilt.

Question 6.9

BRIDGES and JONES were both suspected of committing a murder. During police interviews they exercised their right to silence. There was other evidence and they were charged. The senior investigating officer (SIO) was concerned that the evidence was flimsy and wanted confession evidence from the suspects. Aware that no further interviews were allowed the SIO concocted a ruse where the custody officer argued with the SIO in front of the suspects claiming he had to place them both in the same cell. The SIO apologised to the suspects claiming the custody officer was an 'arse for making you share a cell'. The cell was bugged and the suspects engaged in a conversation which contained a number of damaging admissions, and was recorded.

Considering the evidence obtained during the bugged conversation, which of the following is correct?

A The evidence is admissible as the police did not trick them into making the admissions.

B The evidence will be admissible, but the police will have to re-interview them to allow them to comment upon it.

C The evidence is not admissible as it was obtained after interview and charge.

D The evidence is not admissible as it was obtained by a cheat, where the custody officer clearly lied to the suspects.

Question 6.10

ALBERTS was in custody together with several family members accused of drug dealing. ALBERTS was represented by RITTER and during consultation ALBERTS asked RITTER to establish if the police would release his family members if he confessed to the drug dealing. Although not promising anything the police told RITTER that the case against the other family members was borderline and if at the end of the inquiry there was insufficient evidence they would be released. This information given by the police was correct. ALBERTS confessed, and was even asked leading questions during the police interview by RITTER, in line with his instructions from ALBERTS. At court ALBERTS wishes to have his confession excluded as it was unfairly obtained, even though it was the truth as he was the actual drug dealer.

In relation to this application, which of the following is correct?

A The confession should stand as it was not unreliable.

B The confession should stand as it was true and not gained by oppression.

C The confession should be excluded as it was based on the premise that, if given, family members would be released.

D The confession should be excluded as RITTER was negligent in assisting ALBERTS' confession by asking questions.

Question 6.11

BENTHAM is accused of indecent assault on two male youths. His defence is that the youths' mother put them up to making the allegation after he turned down her sexual advances towards him. He maintains he is heterosexual despite the fact that during a lawfully conducted search of his house several homosexual magazines were found. The defence ask that the magazines be excluded from evidence.

Is it likely that the evidence of the magazines will be admitted?

A Yes, the evidence was obtained by a lawful search of the premises, not unfairly obtained.

B Yes, the evidence is being used to counter an assertion made by the defendant, not as evidence of the offence.

C No, it is not direct evidence and is likely to have an adverse effect on the fairness of the trial.

D No, although it is direct evidence it is likely to have an adverse effect on the fairness of the trial.

Question 6.12

LARK is an undercover officer working on a drugs operation. The police are carrying out an operation on XHOSH, a known drug dealer. LARK is authorised (proper authorities for this operation have been obtained) to purchase drugs from XHOSH. He approaches XHOSH who offers to sell him a wrap of amphetamine. LARK hands over the money and takes the drugs. During the transaction LARK asks XHOSH if he can supply a firearm for a robbery he is planning. XHOSH agrees to this and plans a later meeting.

In relation to LARK's request, which of the following is true?

A This is not entrapment as XHOSH is volunteering to get the firearm.

B This is not entrapment as the undercover operation has been authorised.

C This may be entrapment as LARK is no longer a passive observer.

D This is entrapment as LARK was not authorised by the operation to buy firearms.

Question 6.13

Police officers are carrying out an undercover operation involving drug supply. BEAT-TIE mistakes one of the undercover officers for a drug supplier and approaches him and asks if he can supply heroin to him. The officer agrees to such supply in order to preserve his cover. Other officers arrest BEATTIE for encouraging or assisting in the commission of an offence. He denies this and argues that the officer could not have been encouraged to commit an offence as the police have defences to drug possession; he also argues that it was impossible for the officer to supply heroin.

Given this is an undercover police operation, which of the following is correct?

A This could be seen as entrapment as the officer agrees to supply the drugs.

B The fact BEATTIE approached an undercover police officer means the officer cannot have committed an offence.

C The fact that the officer could not actually supply drugs means BEATTIE cannot commit an offence.

D BEATTIE can commit the offence, it would be possible for the officer to supply the drugs.

ANSWERS

Answer 6.1

Answer **C** — In ensuring that a person has a fair trial the court may exclude evidence, even though the evidence itself is admissible. The court may exclude any evidence in certain circumstances and has additional powers in relation to evidence obtained by confession. The courts' powers to exclude evidence come generally from s. 78 of the Police and Criminal Evidence Act 1984 (and specifically in relation to confession evidence from s. 76(2) of that Act), although the courts also have common law powers to exclude evidence.

This is supported by s. 76A of the Police and Criminal Evidence Act 1984 which states that as long as it has not been excluded by the court under s. 76A (which makes similar provisions for exclusion as those under s. 76), in any proceedings where a confession was made by one accused person it may be given in evidence for another person charged in the same proceedings (a co-accused); answer D is therefore incorrect.

The key part of this subsection is that the co-accused must be 'charged in the same proceedings', for instance in *R* v *Finch* [2007] EWCA Crim 36 where one suspect pleaded guilty the House of Lords held that he was no longer a person charged or accused in the trial, accordingly s. 76A of the 1984 Act did not apply and what he said to the police was not admissible; answer B is therefore incorrect.

It is correct to say that he is a witness, however, he would have to give evidence-in-chief, and a previous confession made on tape would NOT be admissible as outlined in *Finch*; answer A is therefore incorrect.

Evidence and Procedure, para. 2.6.2.1

Answer 6.2

Answer **C** — Section 78 of the Police and Criminal Evidence Act 1984 states:

(1) In any proceedings the court may refuse to allow evidence on which the prosecution proposes to rely to be given if it appears to the court that, having regard to all the circumstances, including the circumstances in which the evidence was obtained, the admission of the evidence would have such an adverse effect on the fairness of the proceedings that the court ought not to admit it.

The important question here is, what is the actual evidence obtained? The answer is that it is the DNA obtained from the hair, not the hair itself. So although the officer's actions clearly breached the Police and Criminal Evidence Act 1984 Codes of Practice (and are reprehensible) the obtaining of the actual evidence (DNA) did not breach the codes. If a sample of hair is obtained by an assault and not in accordance with ss. 63 and 65 of the 1984 Act and is then used to prepare a DNA profile which implicates the accused, the evidence will be admitted on the basis that the means used to obtain it have done nothing to cast doubt on its reliability and strength (see *R* v *Cooke* [1995] 1 Cr App R 318); answers A and B are therefore incorrect.

Any physical evidence found should be excluded, however, where there is a real risk that the improper means used to obtain it have affected its reliability, and therefore the fairness of the trial, for example a case involving a complete flouting of Code B in which the accused claims that the property allegedly found must have been planted; answer D is therefore incorrect.

Evidence and Procedure, para. 2.6.3.1

Answer 6.3

Answer **A** — Section 82(3) of the Police and Criminal Evidence Act 1984 retained the courts' common law power to exclude evidence at their discretion.

For evidence to be excluded at common law the court will not so much concern itself with *how* evidence is obtained, but rather the *effect* that the evidence will have at trial; answer B is therefore incorrect as this reverses this doctrine.

Evidence can be excluded at common law at any time during the trial, including pre-trial submissions (*voir dire*) so it can be excluded prior to evidence even being presented; answer D is therefore incorrect.

In these cases the courts are looking at the trial process itself, as opposed to the investigation, and therefore this power has less impact on how investigations should be conducted therefore breaches of the Codes of Practice have limited effect here; answer C is therefore incorrect.

Evidence and Procedure, para. 2.6.3.3

Answer 6.4

Answer **C** — This question shows what could happen where vital evidence is lost due to police impropriety (i.e. a clear inducement to confess), particularly where a false pretence has been used. The first interview was rightly excluded, and for the same reasons it is more than likely that the second interview would also be excluded. Answers A and D are therefore incorrect. In this case, it will not be possible to show any connection between the suspect and the weapon and, unless there is some other evidence to link the weapon to the suspect, the case may fail. The reason is that it would not be possible to say that the police went to the location where the weapon was hidden without at least implying that the suspect had indicated that it was there when interviewed, and answer B is therefore incorrect. All that can be said is that the weapon was found at the particular location, which could be accessible to any number of people, and that the scientific evidence shows it to be the murder weapon.

Evidence and Procedure, paras 2.6.2.5, 2.6.2.6

Answer 6.5

Answer **B** — A 'confession' is defined by s. 82 of the 1984 Act, which states:

> In this Part of this Act—'confession' includes any statement wholly or partly adverse to the person who made it, whether made to a person in authority or not and whether made in words or otherwise; . . .

So a confession can be made to a person not in authority; answer A is therefore incorrect.

So is the confession reliable and admissible? A defendant was told by his employer that if he admitted to the theft no further action would be taken, but if he did not admit it, the employer would contact the police. The suspect admitted it; nevertheless the employer called the police. The manager's untrue inducement to the defendant made his confession unreliable, therefore the confession had been wrongfully admitted, which rendered the conviction unsafe (*R v Roberts* [2011] EWCA Crim 2974); answer C is therefore incorrect.

A significant statement is one which appears to be capable of being used in evidence, and in particular a direct admission of guilt, so as this statement could not be used (as per *Roberts*) answer D is therefore incorrect.

Evidence and Procedure, paras 2.6.2, 2.6.2.6

Answer 6.6

Answer **D** — In some cases where the suspect initially confesses to the offence, he/she may still plead not guilty, alleging that the confession was obtained by oppression and/or in circumstances that would render it unreliable or that it should be excluded as having been unfairly obtained. The courts are concerned with the reliability of evidence and often regard confessions as the least reliable way to prove a person's involvement in an offence.

A court is under a duty to exclude a confession where it has been, or may have been, obtained by the oppression of the person making the confession.

Where an issue has been raised about the veracity of the confession it will be for the prosecution to satisfy the judge that the confession was made voluntarily; even where the confession is admissible a jury would still need to be directed that they should disregard the confession if they considered that it was or may have been obtained by oppression or in consequence of anything said or done that was likely to render it unreliable (*R v Mushtaq* [2005] UKHL 25).

So, if the issue is raised the judge will consider whether it was made voluntarily and should be admitted in evidence but will warn the jury to disregard it if they consider it was obtained by oppression or other unfair means; answers A, B and C are therefore incorrect.

Evidence and Procedure, para. 2.6.2.4

Answer 6.7

Answer **A** — The issue of entrapment falls into two categories: that is to say, trying to obtain evidence relating to offences that have already been committed; and those cases where evidence is obtained of offences yet to be committed. In relation to offences yet to be committed, the key question is whether the suspects voluntarily applied themselves to 'the trick' and that they were not enticed or provoked into committing a crime which they would otherwise not have committed. In *R v Jones* [2007] EWCA Crim 1118 the police had received reports of graffiti being written in black marker on the toilets of trains and stations seeking girls of 8 to 13 years old for sex, offering payment and leaving a contact number. In *Jones* police began an undercover operation using an officer posing as a 12-year-old girl. The undercover officer exchanged several texts with the suspect which clarified her age and arrangements for a meeting. The defendant sent the officer further text messages of an explicit nature including various sexual acts that he expected he would be able to perform on her. The Court of Appeal held that the police did not incite or instigate a crime but merely provided the opportunity for the defendant to commit a similar offence and provide evidence for a conviction. The fact that the officer is acting with a false persona on a social media site is acceptable with the relevant authorisation; answer D is therefore incorrect. The officer did no more than pretend to be a child of a particular age. The police did not behave improperly in choosing the age of 12. In the scenario of this question it was BLOUNT who had asked the officer for her age, and he therefore believed that he was inciting penetrative sexual activity with a child under 13.

BLOUNT is charged with an attempt to commit the offence, and the message in the toilet would not be 'more than merely preparatory'; however, the police action is certainly more than an attempt just to locate him, and is part of evidence gathering; for these reasons, answer B is incorrect. As the offence charged is 'attempt' it is irrelevant that the actual offence could not have been committed; answer C is therefore incorrect.

Evidence and Procedure, para. 2.6.3.4

Answer 6.8

Answer **D** — Section 82(1) of the Police and Criminal Evidence Act 1984 makes it clear that the law is no longer concerned with whether a confession was made to a person in authority, such as a police or customs officer, and that the statutory test for admissibility is equally applicable to, for example, an informal admission to a friend or colleague. Answer A is therefore incorrect.

When the case against a defendant in a joint trial depended on the prosecution proving the guilt of a co-defendant, and the evidence against the co-defendant consisted solely of their own out-of-court confession, then that confession would be admissible against the defendant but only insofar as it went to proving the co-defendant's guilt. At the end of the prosecution case the defendant would have a case to answer, because the jury could properly find, first, that the co-defendant was guilty on the basis of their own confession, and then go on to find that the fact of the co-defendant's guilt coupled with any other evidence incriminating the defendant was sufficient to prove the latter's guilt.

This was the finding by a 3:2 majority judgment in the House of Lords in *R v Hayter* [2005] UKHL 6, despite the general principle that a confession is relevant and admissible only against its maker. Therefore answers B and C are incorrect.

Evidence and Procedure, para. 2.6.2

Answer 6.9

Answer **A** — So what have the police done? They lied to the suspects that they had to be put into the same cell. Although this was an untruthful act by the police did it lead directly to any evidence being obtained because of those lies?

In *R v Bailey; R v Smith* [1993] Crim LR 681 a blatant piece of play acting was approved. The investigating officers and the custody officer played out a conversation in front of the defendants, in which the custody officer, appearing to act against the wishes of the investigating officers, insisted on placing the two defendants in the same cell. In fact, the investigating officers wanted the defendants together, as the cell was bugged. The defendants, lulled into a false sense of security, engaged in a conversation which contained a number of damaging admissions, and was recorded. The Court of Appeal found nothing wrong in what the police had done, even though it was clearly a means of circumventing the fact that they could not question the defendants further (because they had both already been charged). The court held that the fact the defendants could not, under Code of Practice C, properly have been subjected to further questioning did not mean that they had to be protected from the opportunity to speak incriminatingly to one another if they chose to do so. It was acknowledged to appear odd that, alongside the 'rigorously controlled legislative regime' for questioning it should be considered acceptable for 'parallel covert investigations' legitimately to continue, but, provided such stratagems were used only in grave cases and that there was no suggestion of oppression or unreliability, there was nothing unfair about admitting the evidence obtained in consequence.

The evidence will be adduced; answers B, C and D are therefore incorrect.

Evidence and Procedure, para. 2.6.3.1

Answer 6.10

Answer **A** — Section 76(2) of the Police and Criminal Evidence Act 1984 gives the courts a responsibility to exclude confessions where they have been obtained by oppression (s. 76(2)(a)), or where the court considers they are unreliable (s. 76(2)(b)). There is also a general power (under s. 78 of the 1984 Act and at common law) to exclude any evidence that the court considers would be detrimental to the fairness of the trial if allowed, which can also be applicable to the exclusion of confessions. When looking at whether a confession is reliable, the court will consider the circumstances as they actually were at the time and not as they were believed to be. The circumstances are that the family members would be released if there was no evidence against them. This was not a condition of a confession; answer C is therefore incorrect.

In relation to s. 76(2), the court is more concerned about the circumstances in which the confession was obtained than the truthfulness of what was said. So even though it is the truth and not gained by oppression, if the court feels that the way the confession was gained was unfair it may exclude it; answer B is therefore incorrect.

It is the duty of a solicitor to give rational help and advice to their client, and to carry out their instructions. Their client can hardly cry foul if the solicitor follows this edict; answer D is therefore incorrect.

Evidence and Procedure, para. 2.6.2.4

Answer 6.11

Answer **C** — The question that is important here is what is the charge? In this case, it is indecent assault, so any evidence adduced by the prosecution must relate to the facts in issue. Such facts will include:

- the identity of the defendant;
- the *actus reus*;
- the *mens rea*.

In what way will the magazines assist here? The fact is they don't and their prejudicial effect is likely to far outweigh their probative value, particularly as their probative value seems to be little if anything (taking the facts in issue into account).

The court may refuse to allow evidence on which the prosecution proposes to rely if it appears to the court that, having regard to all the circumstances, including the circumstances in which the evidence was obtained, the admission of the evidence would have such an adverse effect on the fairness of the proceedings that the court ought not to admit it.

This is all the circumstances not just those in which the evidence was obtained, so although it was not unfairly obtained it may still be excluded; answer A is therefore incorrect.

Just because a defendant makes an assertion in their defence does not allow the prosecution to adduce evidence to counter that, the prejudicial/probative test will always be applied; answer B is therefore incorrect.

The magazines do not represent direct evidence of the crime charged; answer D is therefore incorrect.

Of course whether evidence is excluded is a matter for the court, however, you were asked if it was likely it would be admitted. In this case, it is unlikely as the scenario mirrors *R* v *B (RA)* [1997] 2 Cr App R 88 where the evidence was excluded.

Evidence and Procedure, para. 2.6.3.1

Answer 6.12

Answer **D** — Police entrapment occurs when a law enforcer such as a police constable causes a person to commit an offence with the intention of prosecution for that offence. (For example, posing, or hiring someone to pose as a street prostitute and waiting for a 'kerb crawler' to attempt to solicit for the services of the prostitute from their vehicle.) Therefore, the key issue in an application for a stay of proceedings on the grounds of abuse of process or exclusion of evidence under s. 78 of the Police and

Criminal Evidence Act 1984 in entrapment cases is the conduct of the police or the prosecuting authority. There has to be some kind of criticism to be levelled specifically at the police or the Crown Prosecution Service relating to how the evidence was obtained, without this impropriety any argument regarding exclusion of evidence or an abuse of process is likely to fail. In this scenario the criticism is that the officer went beyond the brief for the operation and therefore it was an abuse of process. Sometimes the lines can be blurred in these cases as to what is or is not entrapment, in this scenario however the abuse of process is clear; the officer has asked the suspect to commit an offence completely unrelated to the operation the officer is undercover for and such is clear entrapment; answers A, B and C are therefore incorrect.

Evidence and Procedure, para. 2.6.4

Answer 6.13

Answer **D** — One of the arguments that is often raised by defendants who are caught by undercover officers is that they were induced or pressurised into committing the offence by the officers and that, as a result, either they should not be prosecuted or the evidence of the officer(s) should be excluded. This is mostly true where the approach is made by the officers to the suspect. And it is in this area only that entrapment is likely to occur; where the suspect approaches the officer, the officer cannot 'entrap' someone who voluntarily looks to commit an offence; answer A is therefore incorrect.

What of the situation where, rather than approaching others, an undercover police officer is approached to take part in a proposed offence? There are several types of situation where this may occur.

In relation to this activity, there is no need for the person encouraged to have any intention of going on to commit the offence. The Divisional Court has held that there is no requirement for 'parity of *mens rea*' between the parties (*DPP* v *Armstrong* [2000] Crim LR 379). In that case the defendant had approached an undercover police officer asking him to supply child pornography. At his trial, the defendant argued that, as the officer in reality had no intention of supplying the pornography, there was no offence of incitement (now encouraging/assisting an offence). On appeal by the prosecutor, the Divisional Court held that incitement, like conspiracies and attempts, was an ancillary offence where criminal liability was attributed to the defendant where the full offence had not been committed. Consequently the intent of the person incited was irrelevant. The court also held that the issue of impossibility did not arise in circumstances such as Armstrong's because it had been 'possible' for the officer to supply the material; answers B and C are therefore incorrect.

Evidence and Procedure, para. 2.6.4

7 Disclosure of Evidence

STUDY PREPARATION

Once again, this is an area that began life as a common law development through the courts, being later encapsulated in statute—the Criminal Procedure and Investigations Act 1996 (as amended by the Criminal Justice Act 2003).

Although most of the specific responsibilities under the Act fall on the disclosure officer, the general duties of the disclosure system are important to all police officers and others involved in the gathering of evidence.

As well as understanding the main principles of the Criminal Procedure and Investigations Act—and the code that accompanies it—you should also understand the practical aspects of disclosure schedules, defence statements and retention of materials.

QUESTIONS

Question 7.1

Constable STEYN was investigating a fraud case, and had taken several statements. He spoke to one particular witness, ROGERS, who claimed that another witness, MURPHY, may not possibly have seen what she said she had seen. ROGERS claims MURPHY did not like the defendant as she had been rude to her previously. However, there is no evidence that MURPHY is lying in her statement and it's only ROGERS' opinion. The officer recorded this in his pocket notebook. All the statements taken indicate that the defendant passed cheques fraudulently and it was captured on CCTV.

In relation to disclosure which of the following is correct in relation to the officer's pocket notebook note?

A As there is no evidence that MURPHY may be mistaken in what she saw, the note does not have to be disclosed.

B As there is other compelling evidence, including CCTV, this note does not have to be disclosed.

C The note would have to be disclosed as it relates to the investigation and has been recorded.

D The note would have to be disclosed as it indicates a possible motive for lying by a witness.

Question 7.2

Police officers have received intelligence to suggest that an armed robbery will take place at a local post office. They set up lawful surveillance on a post office, but after a day that is withdrawn as they have intelligence to suggest that HOUSE is the suspect and the surveillance moves on to him.

Regarding the surveillance at the post office, which of the following is correct in relation to material obtained during that surveillance in line with the Criminal Procedure and Investigations Act 1996 and its definition of 'criminal investigation'?

A All the material from the investigation/operation would need to be retained and disclosed if necessary, including the location of the surveillance.

B All the material from the investigation/operation would have to be reviewed to see if it is relevant to the defence case.

C All the material from the investigation/operation is not relevant as at that time a crime had not been committed.

D All the material from the investigation/operation is not relevant as at that time a suspect had not been identified.

Question 7.3

Police officers have been carrying out covert surveillance in relation to the large-scale supply of Class A drugs. They have used undercover officers and a CHIS (covert human intelligence source) and these people are clearly visible on the recorded footage. The defence have asked for this material, which was deemed to be sensitive by the prosecutor, to be made available to them.

In relation to this which of the following is correct?

A The court would decide if 'public interest immunity' applied. If it did, the material need not be disclosed.

B As the material has been considered to be sensitive, it can only be disclosed if the 'public interest immunity' test fails or with the express written approval of the Attorney General.

C As the material has been considered to be sensitive, it can only be disclosed if the 'public interest immunity' test fails or with the express written approval of the Director of Public Prosecutions.

D As the material has been considered to be sensitive, it need not be disclosed, unless the prohibitive value of it to the defence outweighed the prejudicial effect it would have on the person seen in it.

Question 7.4

KENDAL has been charged with murder, and is awaiting committal to the Crown Court.

In relation to the unused evidential material held by the prosecution, how much, if any, needs to be disclosed prior to committal to ensure KENDAL's right to a fair trial?

A All of the unused material must be disclosed, or the case may be halted as an abuse of process.

B Some of the material should be disclosed at an early stage (e.g. information to assist a bail application).

C None of the material, as the Criminal Procedure and Investigations Act 1996 requires disclosure after committal only.

D Most of the material should be disclosed, except that material which has been deemed to be 'sensitive'.

Question 7.5

GREIG has been charged with an indictable offence and has been committed to Crown Court. He intends calling a number of defence witnesses to give evidence at court.

In relation to this which of the following is correct?

A The defence must indicate that they are calling witnesses other than the accused.

B The defence must indicate that they are calling witnesses, and identify them, other than the accused.

C The defence only have to indicate whether the defendant will be giving evidence or not.

D The defence are under no obligation to provide any details of defence witnesses.

Question 7.6

RICHLEY has been charged with an offence of fraud and the prosecution has given initial disclosure. The case will be tried in the Crown Court and the defence are preparing a defence statement.

Which of the following is correct in relation to what should be in that statement?

A Only the nature of the defence case is required at this stage.

B The nature of the defence case and any witnesses only.

C The nature of the defence case, witnesses and details of any alibi only.

D The nature of the defence case, witnesses, details of any alibi and any point of law to be raised.

Question 7.7

LICARI is giving evidence at the Crown Court as a prosecution witness. During LICARI's evidence-in-chief, she gives evidence which is materially inconsistent with the first statement she made earlier to the police. In her first statement to the police LICARI stated that she had seen the accused at the place where the crime was committed about three hours before the crime was committed. This statement was contained in the schedule of unused material, but was not disclosed by the prosecution as it did not undermine their case. It is on her second statement to the police, which was disclosed, that she is now giving evidence.

What should the prosecution now do in relation to the first statement?

A Nothing, as disclosure rules ceased to apply when the trial began.

B Nothing, as the statement only supports the prosecution case, it does not undermine it.

C The prosecution should ensure it is retained in case of any future appeal.

D The prosecution should disclose it immediately so that the defence can use it in cross-examination to discredit the testimony of the witness.

Question 7.8

Detective Sergeant BARRY was the disclosure officer on a particularly complex fraud case; unfortunately he broke his leg playing rugby and is unable to continue in his role as disclosure officer on the case. The case is nearing the stage where further disclosure is to be made.

At this stage who is responsible for assigning a new disclosure officer?

A Detective Sergeant BARRY's first line manager.

B Detective Sergeant BARRY's first line manager, or the police officer in charge of the investigation.

C Detective Sergeant BARRY's first line manager, or the police officer in charge of the investigation in consultation with the Crown Prosecution Service.

D The prosecutor from the Crown Prosecution Service who is in direct charge of the investigation.

Question 7.9

During a police investigation into a street robbery, a key eyewitness provides a statement outlining in detail the description of the attacker. When the robber is eventually captured, he admits the offence on audio-recorded interview and there is ample supporting evidence to show he is guilty. The key eyewitness's description, however, is completely different from the actual appearance of the accused.

Which of the following is true in relation to whether this statement should be included on the schedule and disclosed?

A The prosecution should disclose it if the disclosure officer considers it undermines the prosecution case.

B The prosecution should disclose it only if the prosecutor considers it undermines the prosecution case.

C The prosecution should disclose it only if the prosecutor and the disclosure officer agree it undermines the prosecution case.

D The prosecution should disclose it even if no one involved in the process considers it undermines the prosecution case.

Question 7.10

Constable GUZMAN is engaged in inquiries into an allegation of assault against BANDRICK. Constable GUZMAN obtains a statement from a witness that indicates that BANDRICK was not the person responsible for the assault.

What action best outlines Constable GUZMAN's responsibility as an investigator in relation to this witness statement as required by the Code of Practice under the Criminal Procedure and Investigations Act 1996?

A He should retain the statement and include it on the relevant sensitive material schedule.

B He should retain the statement and disclose it himself as it undermines the prosecution case.

C He should carry out further investigation to gather more evidence that would assist the defence.

D He should inform the prosecutor and seek guidance as to the correct procedure to follow.

Question 7.11

Constable DIMECH received anonymous information that stolen vehicles were being hidden in a garage. She attended the area one evening with Detective Constable COLE in an unmarked police vehicle, which they used to keep observation on the garage. They saw PARNIS pull up in a Range Rover and they approached him to question him about the car. On seeing them, he sped off and was lost. PARNIS was traced two days later and was lawfully arrested. This was witnessed by NEACHELL. Constable DIMECH became the disclosure officer, and subsequently discovered that Detective Constable COLE was under investigation by the complaints department for giving false evidence in court in a recent case.

In relation to material that needs to be disclosed to the defence, which of the following is correct?

A A statement would have to be obtained from NEACHELL and disclosed to the defence.

B The investigation against Detective Constable COLE may have to be disclosed, even though he has not been convicted.

C The details of the police vehicle used for the observation would not need to be disclosed.

D As the anonymous information is inadmissible as evidence, the fact of its existence does not need to be conveyed to the prosecutor.

Question 7.12

The Criminal Procedure and Investigations Act 1996 outlines what statements should be disclosed in cases that involve complaints against police officers. MOTHERSOLE is the father of a youth who has made a complaint of assault against a police officer. He is aware that the police have obtained several witness statements.

In relation to these statements which of the following is correct?

A MOTHERSOLE is entitled at any time to have those statements disclosed to him.

B MOTHERSOLE is entitled at any time to have those statements disclosed to him, at the earliest opportunity but at the conclusion of the investigation.

C MOTHERSOLE is not entitled to any disclosure as he is not the actual complainant.

D MOTHERSOLE is only entitled to disclosure if criminal charges are raised against the police officer.

Question 7.13

Police have been investigating drug supply and as such have been using a disused office premises nearby as an observation post. During the trial the defence ask that the jury be taken to the observation post to test what the officers could see and as such they are seeking to have the location of the observation post disclosed.

In relation to this which of the following is correct?

A The location would have to be disclosed as there are no grounds to withhold it.

B The location would have to be disclosed as it is not a private house.

C The location need not be disclosed if there is fear or threat of violence.

D The location need not be disclosed if there is fear or threat of harassment.

Question 7.14

EAST appeared in Crown Court as a defendant for an offence of robbery. Before the trial, EAST's solicitor served a defence statement on the prosecution, outlining an alibi for the offence, which the police were able to negate. EAST elected to give evidence on his own behalf during the trial and, under cross-examination, he put forward a different alibi to the offence. As a result, the prosecuting barrister sought permission from the court to examine EAST about the contents of his defence statement.

Could the prosecution's request be granted in these circumstances?

A No, under no circumstances may a defendant be cross-examined in relation to a defence statement.

B Yes, the request may be granted in these circumstances.

C No, a defendant may be cross-examined in relation to a defence statement only when he or she is accused of an offence of perjury.

D Yes, a defendant may be cross-examined in relation to a defence statement on every occasion.

Question 7.15

PRODAN has been charged with attempted rape and has been committed for trial. The disclosure officer, Detective Constable LANE, has discovered a previous allegation of crime made against the complainant in the attempted rape case, which indicated that she was a prostitute and that she had stolen from the male who had made this complaint. Detective Constable LANE discovered that the male who made this previous allegation had given false details and could not be traced; this crime had in fact been 'no crimed'.

Should this previous unsubstantiated crime complaint be disclosed under the Criminal Procedure and Investigations Act 1996?

A This should be disclosed as it is relevant material.

B This should be disclosed as it undermines the prosecution case.

C This should not be disclosed as it was a false allegation.

D This should not be disclosed as it was not recorded as a crime and is not therefore relevant material.

Question 7.16

ROGERS and BARBU were jointly charged with fraud relating to counterfeit computer software from a major software company. The police are aware that there was material in the hands of the major software company that may be prejudicial to the prosecution case; however, as the company is American they cannot get hold of the material, and they have never inspected it.

What is their liability in relation to disclosure of this material to the defence?

A The prosecutor must obtain the material, or risk the prosecution being stayed.

B The prosecutor must disclose to the defence why they think the material may be prejudicial.

C The prosecutor is under no duty to disclose material that has not come into their hands.

D The prosecutor must take all reasonable steps to obtain the material.

Question 7.17

VESELY has been charged with an offence of causing death by dangerous driving and will be appearing before the Crown Court. The prosecution has given initial disclosure; and the defence provided a defence statement 22 days after the initial disclosure.

Which of the following is correct in relation to what the prosecution must now do?

A Consider the impact of the defence statement in terms of the need for any further disclosure, it was submitted in time.

B Consider the impact of the defence statement in terms of the need for any further disclosure, even though it was submitted outside the statutory 14-day period allowed.

C Consider the impact of the defence statement in terms of the need for any further disclosure, even though it was submitted outside the statutory 21-day period allowed.

D Consider the statement, but as it is late they are no longer under an obligation to provide further disclosure, that is now voluntary.

ANSWERS

Answer 7.1

Answer **D** — Disclosure by the prosecutor is covered by s. 3 of the Criminal Procedure and Investigations Act 1996. This section talks about material which 'might undermine the prosecution case against the accused'. Such material will consist mainly of material which raises questions over the strength of the prosecution case, the value of evidence given by witnesses and issues relating to identification. If officers feel that the material is not relevant to the prosecution case but may be useful to the defence in cross-examination, it may well come within the category of material which undermines the prosecution case. This is the test, not the fact that the evidence has been recorded; answer C is therefore incorrect.

In *Tucker* v *Crown Prosecution Service* [2008] EWCA Crim 3063, the prosecution never revealed to the defence the record containing important information as to a possible motive for a witness lying about the defendant's involvement in the offence, which led to the conviction being overturned. This was clearly material that undermined the prosecution case as it raised questions over the value of the witness's evidence. There does not need to be compelling evidence of this and the fact that there is other evidence supporting the prosecution case does not undermine this duty; answers A and B are therefore incorrect.

Evidence and Procedure, para. 2.7.6.3

Answer 7.2

Answer **B** — The Criminal Procedure and Investigations Act 1996 is primarily concerned with the disclosure of material which does not form part of the prosecution case resulting from a criminal investigation (i.e. 'unused material'). A criminal investigation is defined by s. 1(4) of the 1996 Act and para. 2.1 of the Code of Practice. In order to satisfy the disclosure requirements police officers should consider recording and retaining material in the early stages of an investigation. This will include:

- investigations into crimes that have been committed;
- investigations the purpose of which is to ascertain whether a crime has been committed, with a view to the possible institution of criminal proceedings; and
- investigations which begin in the belief that a crime may be committed, for example when the police keep premises or individuals under observation for a period of

time, with a view to the possible institution of criminal proceedings; answer C is therefore incorrect.

In these cases the investigation may well have started some time before the defendant became a suspect; answer D is therefore incorrect. In such cases all the material from the investigation/operation would have to be reviewed to see if it is relevant to the defence case. In cases where there is a surveillance operation or observation point, it may be that the details of the observation point and the surveillance techniques would not be revealed but it would be necessary to retain material generating from it; answer A is therefore incorrect.

Evidence and Procedure, para. 2.7.5

Answer 7.3

Answer **A** — This is material which the investigator believes it is not in the public interest to disclose. While the general principle that governs the 1996 Act and Art. 6 of the European Convention is that material should not be withheld from the defence, sensitive material is an exception to this. In *Van Mechelen* v *Netherlands* [1997] 25 EHRR 647, the court stated that in some cases it may be necessary to withhold certain evidence from the defence so as to preserve the fundamental rights of another individual or to safeguard an important public interest; this is the test and although probative value/prejudicial effect are factors, the public interest test extends beyond this; answer D is therefore incorrect. However, only such measures restricting the rights of the defence which are strictly necessary are permissible under Art. 6. It should be noted that the court did recognise that the entitlement of disclosure of relevant evidence was not an absolute right but could only be restricted as was strictly necessary. In *R* v *Keane* [1994] 1 WLR 746 Lord Taylor CJ stated that:

> the judge should carry out a balancing exercise, having regard both to the weight of the public interest in non-disclosure and to the importance of the documents to the issues of interest, present and potential, to the defence, and if the disputed material might prove a defendant's innocence or avoid a miscarriage of justice, the balance came down resoundingly in favour of disclosure.

Decisions as to what should be withheld from the defence are a matter for the court and where necessary an application to withhold the material must be made to the court (*R* v *Ward* [1993] 1 WLR 619). The application of public interest immunity was considered by the House of Lords in *R* v *H* [2004] UKHL 3. In this case the defendants were charged with conspiracy to supply a Class A drug following a covert police investigation, and sought disclosure of material held by the prosecution relating to the investigation. The prosecution resisted the disclosure on grounds of public interest immunity. The court held that if the material did not weaken the prosecution case or strengthen the defence, there would be no requirement to disclose it. Only in truly borderline cases should the prosecution seek a judicial ruling on the disclosability of material in their hands. In considering any disclosure issue the trial judge had constantly to bear in mind the overriding principle that derogation from the principle of full disclosure had always to be the minimum necessary to protect the public interest in question and must never imperil the overall fairness of the trial. Once material is considered to be sensitive then it should be disclosed only if the public interest application fails (unless abandoning the case is considered more appropriate) or with the express written approval of the Treasury Solicitor; answers B and C are therefore incorrect (CPS Disclosure Manual, Chapters 33/34).

Evidence and Procedure, para. 2.7.9.3

Answer 7.4

Answer **B** — There has always been an ethical dimension to the duty to disclose, and the decision in *R* v *DPP, ex parte Lee* [1999] 1 WLR 1950 is an indication that it survives the introduction of the Criminal Procedure and Investigations Act 1996. In *Lee*, the Divisional Court considered whether the prosecution had a duty to disclose unused material in indictable-only offences prior to committal. The statutory framework for disclosure set out in the 1996 Act is silent as to any such duty until after committal. But there may well be reasons why it would be helpful to the defence to know of unused material at an earlier stage. For example, the following circumstances were considered by the court:

- the previous convictions of the alleged victim when they might be expected to help the defence in a bail application;
- material to help an application to stay proceedings as an abuse of process;
- material to help the defendant's arguments at committal;
- material to help the defendant prepare for trial, e.g. eyewitnesses whom the prosecution did not intend to use.

Kennedy LJ said that a responsible prosecutor might recognise that fairness required that some of this material might be disclosed. Therefore, only some of the material should be disclosed, and answers A, C and D are therefore incorrect.

Evidence and Procedure, para. 2.7.10.2

Answer 7.5

Answer **B** — In proceedings before the Crown Court, where the prosecutor has provided initial disclosure, or purported to, the accused must serve a defence statement on the prosecutor and the court. The accused must also provide details of any witnesses he or she intends to call at the trial; answers A, C and D are therefore incorrect.

Evidence and Procedure, para. 2.7.11.2

Answer 7.6

Answer **D** — The duty on the defence to make disclosure only arises after the prosecution has made the initial disclosure. The disclosure required by the defence is limited to material that they intend to use at trial.

The defence statement should set out the nature of the defendant's defence, including any particular defences on which he/she intends to rely and particulars of the matters of fact on which the defendant intends to rely; this means the defence will need to disclose a factual narrative of their case. The defence statement must indicate any point of law (including any point as to the admissibility of evidence or an abuse of process) which the defendant wishes to raise, and any authority on which he/she intends to rely for that purpose. Where the defence case involves an alibi, the statement must give details of the alibi, including the name and address of any alibi witness. The defence must also give to the court and the prosecutor notice of any witnesses other than the defendant who will be called to give evidence.

So it's all these facts that the defence statement must contain; answers A, B and C are therefore incorrect.

Evidence and Procedure, para. 2.7.11.2

Answer 7.7

Answer **D** — The duty is on the prosecution to continue to review the disclosure of prosecution material right up until the case is completed (acquittal, conviction or discontinuance of the case), and answer A is therefore incorrect. Material must be disclosed if the prosecutor forms the opinion that there is material which might undermine the prosecution case, or might reasonably be expected to assist the accused's defence. Even if the information did not undermine the prosecution case, the material might have to be disclosed, and answer B is therefore incorrect. It is worth asking a number of pertinent questions: Would the previous statement bring the witness's credibility into question? Would this then assist the accused's defence? If the answer to both these questions is 'yes', the prosecutor would have to do more than just retain the information: it would have to be disclosed immediately to allow the defence an opportunity effectively to cross-examine the witness, and answer C is therefore incorrect.

Evidence and Procedure, para. 2.7.11.6

Answer 7.8

Answer **B** — In all cases there must be an officer in charge of the case (OIC) and a disclosure officer.

In the Criminal Procedure and Investigations Act 1996 Code of Practice at para. 3.7 it is outlined that if, during a criminal investigation, the officer in charge of an investigation or disclosure officer for any reason no longer has responsibility for the functions falling to him, either his supervisor or the police officer in charge of investigations within the police force concerned must assign someone else to assume that responsibility. That person's identity must be recorded, as with those initially responsible for these functions in each investigation.

So it can be either the supervisor *or* the police officer in charge of criminal investigations for the police force concerned that has responsibility for reassigning the role, and there is no need to consult the CPS on this matter; answers A, C and D are therefore incorrect.

Evidence and Procedure, para. 2.7.6

Answer 7.9

Answer **D** — Where disclosure is required, the first task is to create a schedule of all *non-sensitive material* which may be relevant to the investigation, and which has been retained by the police but which does not form part of the prosecution case. Once the schedules have been completed, the disclosure officer must decide what material, if any (whether listed on the schedules or not), might undermine the prosecution case. The disclosure officer must draw this information to the attention of the prosecutor and the reasons why he or she believes that the material undermines the prosecution case. In addition to the schedules and copies of material which undermine the prosecution case, the Codes of Practice to the 1996 Act require the disclosure officer to provide a copy of any material, whether or not he or she considers it to undermine the prosecution case.

One example of this would be a record of the first description of a suspect given to the police by a potential witness, whether or not the description differs from that of the alleged offender. Irrespective of any person's opinion, this material would have to be disclosed, and answers A, B and C are incorrect.

Evidence and Procedure, para. 2.7.9.1

Answer 7.10

Answer **C** — Paragraph 3.5 of the Code of Practice to the Criminal Procedure and Investigations Act 1996, requires investigators to pursue all reasonable lines of inquiry, *whether these point towards or away from the suspect*. Although the officer must retain the statement, it would not fit the definition of sensitive material (i.e. material which the investigator believes it is not in the public interest to disclose). Thus, sensitive material does not mean evidence which might harm the prosecution case, and answer A is therefore incorrect. It is the prosecutor's job to disclose the statement, not the police officer's, and answer B is therefore incorrect. Answer D is avoiding the clear responsibility outlined in the Code of Practice and is therefore incorrect.

Evidence and Procedure, para. 2.7.6

Answer 7.11

Answer **B** — What is relevant to the offence, and needs to be disclosed, is a question of fact. In *DPP* v *Metten* [1999] EWHC Admin 49, the court held that the actual arrest for an offence was not relevant to the case as it did not fall within the definition of an investigation in s. 2(1) of the Criminal Procedure and Investigations Act 1996, and answer A is therefore incorrect.

Material obtained during an investigation does not have to be admissible in court for it to undermine the prosecution case (*R* v *Preston* (1994) 98 Cr App R 405), and therefore the anonymous information should form part of the schedule sent to the prosecutor and for that reason answer D is incorrect. Where officers have used an unmarked police vehicle for observation, information relating to the surveillance and the colour, make and model of the vehicle should not be withheld (*R* v *Brown and Daley* [1987] 87 Cr App R 52), and answer C is therefore incorrect. Disclosure of previous convictions and other matters which affect the credibility of the witness, might undermine the prosecution case. Some guidance is given by the case of *R* v *Guney* [1998] 2 Cr App R 242. In *Guney*, the court said that the defence are not entitled to be informed of every occasion when any officer has given evidence 'unsuccessfully', or whenever allegations are made against him or her. However, in this case the court felt that disclosure should have been made. It will therefore be a question of fact in each case, and consultation with the Crown Prosecution Service is advisable if there is any doubt.

Evidence and Procedure, para. 2.7.5.4

Answer 7.12

Answer **B** — Statements made by witnesses during an investigation of a complaint against a police officer are disclosable, however, the timing of the disclosure may be controlled; answer A is therefore incorrect. This is the case even if criminal charges are not raised; answer D is therefore incorrect.

In *R v Police Complaints Authority, ex parte Green* [2002] EWCA Civ 389, the Court of Appeal stated that there is no requirement to disclose witness statements to eyewitness complainants during the course of an investigation. The evidence of such complainants could be contaminated and, therefore, disclosure would risk hindering or frustrating the very purpose of the investigation. A complainant's legitimate interests were appropriately and adequately safeguarded by his or her right to a thorough and independent investigation, to contribute to the evidence, to be kept informed of the progress of the investigation and to be given reasoned conclusions on completion of the investigation. However, a complainant had no right to participate in the investigation as though he or she were supervising it. The general rule was that complainants, whether victims or next of kin, were not entitled to the disclosure of witness statements used in the course of a police investigation until its conclusion at the earliest. Note that disclosure can be made to next of kin; answer C is therefore incorrect.

Evidence and Procedure, para. 2.7.13.2

Answer 7.13

Answer **A** — This question relates to what is known as the *Johnson* ruling. In *R v Johnson* [1988] 1 WLR 1377, the appellant was convicted of supplying drugs. The only evidence against him was given by police officers, who testified that, while stationed in private premises in a known drug-dealing locality, they had observed him selling drugs. The defence applied to cross-examine the officers on the exact location of the observation posts, in order to test what they could see, having regard to the layout of the street and the objects in it. In the jury's absence the prosecution called evidence as to the difficulty of obtaining assistance from the public, and the desire of the occupiers, who were also occupiers at the time of the offence, that their names and addresses should not be disclosed because they feared for their safety.

The judge ruled that the exact location of the premises need not be revealed. This extended the rules established in *R* v *Rankine* [1986] QB 861 (police protecting sources of information) and is based on the protection of the owner or occupier of the premises, and not on the identity of the observation post. Thus, where officers have witnessed the commission of an offence as part of a surveillance operation conducted from an unmarked police vehicle, information relating to the surveillance and the colour, make and model of the vehicle should not be withheld (*R* v *Brown and Daley* (1987) 87 Cr App R 52).

As the observation post was disused, *Johnson* does not apply and no protection can be given (protection could be given even if the premises were business premises, provided there were occupiers); answers B, C and D are therefore incorrect.

Evidence and Procedure, para. 2.7.9.5

Answer 7.14

Answer **B** — This issue was examined in the case of *R* v *Lowe* [2003] EWCA Crim 3182. It was held in this case that there may be occasions where the defence statement is allowed to be used in cross-examination, namely when it is alleged that the defendant has changed his or her defence, or in re-examination to rebut a suggestion of recent invention. Answer A is therefore incorrect.

Such a request will not be granted on every occasion, therefore answer D is incorrect. There is no requirement for the defendant to be facing a charge of perjury, therefore answer C is incorrect.

Evidence and Procedure, para. 2.7.11.1

Answer 7.15

Answer **A** — The Criminal Procedure and Investigations Act 1996 is concerned with the disclosure of material which is obtained during the course of a criminal investigation and which may be relevant to the investigation. Material can be in any form and should be widely interpreted. This applies to any material coming to the knowledge of officers involved in the case at any stage of the investigation or even after a suspect has been charged. This is material which the investigator, officer in charge of the case (OIC) or disclosure officer consider has some bearing on any offence being investigated or any people being investigated for those offences or any of the surrounding circumstances. The material will be relevant whether it is beneficial to the prosecution case, weakens the prosecution case or assists the defence case. It is not only material that will become 'evidence' in the case that should be considered; any information, record or thing which may have a bearing on the case can be material for the purposes of disclosure. The way in which evidence has been obtained in itself may be relevant.

The unsubstantiated crime may not undermine directly the prosecution case, but it is relevant material and ought to be disclosed; answer B is therefore incorrect. In *R v Bourimech* [2002] EWCA Crim 2089 the Court of Appeal held that material concerning false allegations in the past may be relevant material. Indeed in *Bourimech*, where a similar crime complaint was disclosed in a large clip of other documentation (albeit two days before trial) to the defence, and the defence failed to notice it, the appellant's conviction was quashed. The court held that failure to previously disclose the material did amount to an unfairness in the proceedings; answers C and D are therefore incorrect.

Evidence and Procedure, para. 2.7.6.5

Answer 7.16

Answer **C** — Third party material can be considered in two categories:

(a) that which is or has been in the possession of the police or which has been inspected by the police;
(b) all other material not falling under (a).

Material which falls into the first category is covered by the same rules of disclosure as any other material the police have.

In *R v Alibhai* [2004] EWCA Crim 681 the Court of Appeal held that under the Criminal Procedure and Investigations Act 1996 the prosecutor was only under a duty to disclose material in the hands of third parties if that material had come into the prosecutor's hands and the prosecutor was of the opinion that such material undermined the case. However, the Attorney General's Guidelines went further by requiring a prosecutor to take steps pursuing third party disclosure if there was a suspicion that documents would be detrimental to the prosecution or of assistance to the defence. However, in such circumstances, the prosecutor enjoyed a margin of consideration as to what steps were appropriate; answer D is therefore incorrect. The provisions for disclosure are not intended to create duties for third parties to follow. The disclosure duties under the 1996 Act were created in respect of material that the prosecution or the police had and which the prosecution had inspected. There is no risk in having proceedings stayed by not doing all they can to obtain the material and by not having it they cannot be expected to comment on its prejudicial nature; answers A and B are therefore incorrect.

Evidence and Procedure, para. 2.7.6.5

Answer 7.17

Answer **A** — Once the prosecution provides the initial disclosure the defence have 14 days in respect of summary proceedings, or 28 days in respect of Crown Court proceedings within which the accused in criminal proceedings must give a compulsory defence statement under s. 5 of the Act. Although this can be extended by the courts there is no 'leeway' as such; answers B and C are therefore incorrect. However, the courts have held that even if the defence serve the defence statement outside the time limits the prosecution must still consider the impact of the statement in terms of the need for any further disclosure (*Murphy* v *DPP* [2006] EWHC 1753 (Admin)); answer D is therefore incorrect.

Evidence and Procedure, para. 2.7.11.5

8 | Detention and Treatment of Persons by Police Officers

STUDY PREPARATION

The duties imposed by the Police and Criminal Evidence Act 1984 on custody officers are many and various, and, once again, there is no substitute for knowing them in detail. This is a big area, both in terms of its volume and its importance. The need to have custody officers at certain police stations, along with the exceptional circumstances when they will not be needed, are key areas; so too are the basic entitlements of anyone when arrested and brought to a police station.

You will need to know the occasions and grounds on which some of a suspect's entitlements can be delayed and, of course, you will have to know the highly examinable areas of clocks, relevant times and time limits. A complex scenario containing different times, days and locations can often induce panic! However, once you have got the formula for working out the relevant times clear in your mind, detention periods and reviews are very straightforward and questions on them should represent 'easy marks'.

Reviews both before and after charge should be known, as should the areas of searching prisoners, seizing property and the treatment of people in police detention.

QUESTIONS

Question 8.1

Inspector WILKINSON is on duty at a designated police station. There are no sergeants in the custody unit and no other sergeant in the police station is readily available.

In relation to who can perform custody duties in these circumstances which of the following is correct?

A Only an officer of the rank of sergeant may perform the role of custody officer.

B Only an officer of the rank of sergeant may perform the role of custody officer or a constable if a sergeant is not readily available to perform them.

C Inspector WILKINSON can always perform the role of custody officer.

D Inspector WILKINSON can perform the role of custody officer if a sergeant is not readily available to perform them.

Question 8.2

HILL is in custody for a theft offence and has been searched. A number of items are to be retained by the custody officer and HILL is asked to sign the custody record that this is a true record of property. However, HILL refuses to sign the custody record.

Which of the following is correct in relation to Code C of PACE Codes of Practice?

A The custody officer need take no action as there is no requirement for HILL to sign for anything other than his rights.

B The custody officer should just note that HILL refused to sign the custody record.

C The custody officer should note that HILL refused to sign the custody record and the time he refused.

D The custody officer should note that HILL refused to sign the custody record, the time he refused and the reason given for that refusal.

Question 8.3

Constable PETROV has arrested HIGGINS for criminal damage at the inquiry office of a non-designated police station, where she works alone. Constable PETROV intends dealing with HIGGINS at her own station, as he is likely to be in custody only for an hour. Constable PETROV has called for assistance from Constable FRY, who works in a neighbouring station.

Would it be appropriate for Constable PETROV to act as custody officer for HIGGINS in these circumstances?

A Yes, provided she informs an on-duty inspector of her intention.

B No, she is the officer in the case and must await the arrival of Constable FRY, who should act as custody officer.

C Yes, provided she informs an inspector at a designated station of her intention.

D No, HIGGINS may not be dealt with at a non-designated station.

Question 8.4

LEEMAY is in police detention suspected of committing an assault. He was arrested at 3 pm on Monday, he arrived at the police station at 3.30 pm and his detention was authorised at 3.45 pm. Following questioning it has been decided to seek CPS advice as to whether he should be charged; this decision was made at 6 pm.

Given that the police wish to seek CPS advice, when should LEEMAY be released from custody?

A Immediately, there is no power to detain pending CPS advice.

B As soon as advice has been given, but before 3.30 pm on Tuesday.

C As soon as advice has been given, but before 3.45 pm on Tuesday.

D As soon as advice has been given, but before 6 pm on Tuesday.

Question 8.5

HIGGINS is in custody and requests his mother be informed of his arrest. He is later transferred to another police station as the one he was in had a fire and had to be closed. He requests that his girlfriend is informed of his new location.

In relation to this which of the following is correct?

A He has already informed someone of his arrest and he has no right to have someone else informed.

B The person he informed initially must be informed that he has been moved to another police station.

C He can only have his mother informed that he has moved locations, but it will be his choice.

D At the new station he is entitled again to have one person informed of his whereabouts.

Question 8.6

BAKER has been arrested for the theft of a radio from a motor vehicle. BAKER was arrested near the vehicle and was alone. He asks that a friend of his be informed of his arrest and there is no answer. BAKER nominates another friend who also cannot be contacted. He then asks for his mother to be informed, she also does not answer. Finally he asks if his brother can be informed.

In relation to this, which of the following is correct in regard to having someone informed of your whereabouts whilst in police custody.

A BAKER can have his brother informed at the custody officer's discretion.
B The custody officer **must** inform BAKER's brother as PACE requires him to do so.
C The custody officer need not inform the brother as he has made at least two attempts to contact someone.
D The custody officer need not inform the brother as he has made at least three attempts to contact someone.

Question 8.7

MARSHALL has been arrested for murder and arrived at the designated police station at 8 am, his detention was authorised at 8.15 am. Police exercised the right to hold the suspect incommunicado at 9 am. MARSHALL became ill and was taken to hospital where he remained for five hours. During this time he was not questioned about the offence.

By what time, assuming the maximum time allowed is used, will the right to hold the suspect incommunicado end?

A 8 pm the following day, 36 hours after arrival at the police station.
B 8.15 pm the following day, 36 hours after detention was authorised.
C 9 pm the following day, 36 hours after the decision to exercise the right.
D 1 pm the following day, 36 hours after arrival at the police station taking out the five hours not in detention at the hospital.

Question 8.8

O'REILLY has been arrested for armed robbery of a building society, where £50,000 was stolen. The officer in the case has proposed that O'REILLY be denied his right to have someone informed of his arrest, as it may alert his accomplice, who has not yet been arrested. The duty inspector is engaged at a firearms incident, but she can be contacted by mobile phone.

Would it be lawful for the inspector to authorise a delay to O'REILLY's rights over the telephone in these circumstances?

A Yes, but the decision must be recorded in writing within 24 hours.
B No, the authorisation must be given by an officer not below the rank of superintendent.
C Yes, but the decision must be recorded in writing as soon as practicable.
D No, the authorisation must be made in person.

Question 8.9

DAWLISH has been arrested for robbery and has indicated that he wishes legal advice. There is a significant delay in his solicitor attending and he indicated that he would be willing to be interviewed without the solicitor. During the interview his solicitor arrives and the interviewing officer is informed, the interviewing officer has indicated that if the suspect sees his solicitor immediately another suspect may be tipped off. He asks to carry on the interview without a solicitor until the other suspect is identified by DAWLISH.

In these circumstances which of the following is correct?

A In these circumstances the suspect must be allowed to consult with his solicitor immediately; there are no exceptions.

B In these circumstances the interview can continue and the suspect can then be informed that his solicitor has arrived as he stated that he did not require one.

C The consultation with the solicitor can be delayed provided an officer of the rank of inspector or above authorises it.

D The consultation with the solicitor can be delayed provided an officer of the rank of superintendent or above authorises it.

Question 8.10

PRINCE was arrested at 10 am in Reading for an offence of theft. PRINCE arrived at the police station at 10.15 am, when it was discovered that she was wanted for an offence of theft in Bristol. PRINCE was interviewed and charged with theft, and at 3 pm the same day she was taken to Bristol to be interviewed, arriving at the custody office at 4.30 pm.

What would PRINCE's 'relevant time' be, in relation to her detention in Bristol?

A 10 am.

B 3 pm.

C 10.15 am.

D 4.30 pm.

Question 8.11

Inspector WISLICKI is carrying out a review of the detention of a male arrested for a violence offence. The inspector asks if there are any representations the detainee wishes to make about his detention and the detainee starts shouting and swearing at the inspector.

In relation to this which of the following is correct?

A Inspector WISLICKI must listen to the representations unless the detainee is drunk.

B Inspector WISLICKI should listen to the representations even if they are abusive.

C Inspector WISLICKI may refuse to listen to representations from the detainee if the officer considers them unfit to make representations because of their condition or behaviour.

D Inspector WISLICKI may refuse to listen to representations from the detainee if the officer considers them unfit to make representations because of their condition or behaviour but then must take representations from their legal adviser.

Question 8.12

PACE Code C gives guidance as to what a custody officer must record on a custody record when detaining a person with or without charge.

What details should be recorded on the custody record in these circumstances?

A The grounds for detention in the person's presence, unless it is apparent that he or she would not understand what was being said.

B The grounds for detention in the person's presence, regardless of his or her condition.

C The grounds for the person's detention which can be recorded at any time.

D The grounds for detention in the person's presence if it is practicable to do so.

Question 8.13

BROWN, MOTHERSOLE and ROBERTS have been arrested for criminal damage to a shop window. A witness saw one person from the group throwing a stone through the window, but was not able to identify the exact person who caused the damage. BROWN has been interviewed by Constable KEANE, and the officer has asked the custody officer for him to be detained until the other two suspects are interviewed.

Under what circumstances may the custody officer detain BROWN further in these circumstances?

A BROWN may be detained if the custody officer has reasonable grounds to believe it is necessary to preserve evidence.

B BROWN should be released as there is insufficient evidence against him to secure a conviction.

C BROWN may be detained if the custody officer has reasonable cause to suspect it is necessary to preserve evidence.

D BROWN may be detained until the investigation is complete against all three defendants.

Question 8.14

Constable DEAR has attended at a large department store to deal with a person suspected of theft. The officer arrests the person at 3.15 pm and decides to release them on street bail in accordance with s. 30 of the Police and Criminal Evidence Act 1984.

The person is bailed at 3.30 pm to attend at police station 'A' at 6 pm. Unfortunately the person misunderstands the instructions and arrives at police station 'B' which is nearer their home; they arrive at 6 pm.

They are re-directed to police station 'A' arriving at that police station front counter at 6.45 pm in accordance with their bail. They are taken through to the custody unit and detention is authorised at 7.20 pm.

What is the 'relevant time' as outlined in the Police and Criminal Evidence Act 1984?

A 3.30 pm, the time they were bailed.

B 6 pm, the time of arrival at the first police station in that force area.

C 6.45 pm, the time of arrival at the police station to which the notice of bail states they must attend.

D 7.20 pm, the time their detention is authorised.

Question 8.15

STIRLING has been arrested for a summary offence. At 10 pm, Detective Constable MUTKI approached the custody officer, stating that he was not in a position to charge STIRLING and that a vital witness had been identified who would not be available until 9 am the following day. Detective Constable MUTKI asked if a superintendent could authorise STIRLING's continued detention beyond 24 hours in order to speak to the witness. STIRLING has been in custody for 14 hours.

Could a superintendent authorise such a request at this stage of STIRLING's detention?

A Yes, but only after he has been in custody for at least 15 hours.

B No, not until he has been in custody for 24 hours.

C Yes, but only after an inspector has conducted a second review.

D No, as STIRLING has not been arrested for an indictable offence.

Question 8.16

Under ss. 43 and 44 of the Police and Criminal Evidence Act 1984, where a person has been in custody for 36 hours without being charged, the police must apply to a magistrate to extend that person's detention beyond that time.

What is the total amount of detention time that can be authorised by magistrates beyond the original 36 hours, before a person must be charged or released? (Do *not* consider offences under the Terrorism Act 2000.)

A three days.

B 72 hours.

C 36 hours.

D 60 hours.

Question 8.17

WILCE has been in custody for 26 hours, having been detained under the Terrorism Act 2000. A warrant of further detention has been applied for and granted by a magistrate, and WILCE has returned to the custody office.

At what intervals should WILCE now be reviewed in relation to his detention, and who should conduct the reviews?

A There is no requirement to conduct further reviews.

B Reviews should be conducted at least every 12 hours by an inspector.

C Reviews should be conducted at least every nine hours by an inspector.

D Reviews should be conducted at least every 12 hours by a superintendent.

Question 8.18

CROCKER was charged and acquitted of a charge of murder by the Crown Court. Following further inquiries he was arrested under the Criminal Justice Act 2003 for that same murder and is in custody at the police station; CROCKER is not precluded from further prosecution by virtue of s. 75(3) of that Act.

Who is responsible for determining whether there is sufficient evidence to charge CROCKER with murder again?

A The custody officer.

B An officer of at least the rank of superintendent.

C An officer of at least the rank of assistant chief constable (commander in the Metropolitan Police).

D The Director of Public Prosecutions (DPP).

Question 8.19

DE LACY has been arrested for an indictable only offence (the relevant time is 11 pm on Monday) and is in custody at the city centre police station. The superintendent of that police station will be on leave from 1 pm on Tuesday and after that time there will be a rota outlining who the force 'on call' superintendent will be. DE LACY's detention clock will terminate at 11 pm on Tuesday and the officer in charge of the investigation considers that an extension of the detention clock is required; the second review is due at 2 pm on Tuesday.

What must the officer in charge of the investigation do to ensure an extension is granted?

A The superintendent responsible for the city centre police station must authorise the extension prior to terminating duty.

B The superintendent responsible for the city centre police station must authorise the extension prior to terminating duty, so the second review will have to be brought forward.

C The on call superintendent can authorise the extension at any time up to 11 pm on Tuesday.

D The on call superintendent can authorise the extension up to 11 pm on Tuesday but only after the second review.

Question 8.20

THRUSH was arrested for failing to appear at court and is in police custody awaiting court in the morning.

Which of the following is correct in relation to reviews of this detention?

A His detention should be reviewed by an inspector, timings as statutory reviews.

B His detention should be reviewed by the custody officer, timings as statutory reviews.

C His detention should be reviewed by an inspector, periodically.

D His detention should be reviewed by the custody officer, periodically.

Question 8.21

KEY was arrested for affray, and on his arrival at the custody suite he was violent towards the custody officer. KEY was taken to a cell because of his behaviour and, because he had not been searched, the custody officer ordered him to be searched in the cell. The arresting officer, who was female, was present in the cell when KEY was searched by the male custody staff.

Have the provisions of s. 54 of the Police and Criminal Evidence Act 1984 (searching of detained persons) been complied with in these circumstances?

A Yes, a female officer may search a male prisoner, provided it is not an intimate search.

B Yes, provided the female officer did not conduct the search.

C No, the female officer should not have been present at the search.

D Yes, a female officer may search a male prisoner, provided it is not a strip search.

Question 8.22

MURTAGH was arrested and interviewed in relation to a terrorist offence and there is sufficient evidence to charge him. During the interviews MURTAGH was denied access to a solicitor and the charging officer is considering how MURTAGH should be cautioned when charged.

What should the words of this caution be?

A You do not have to say anything. But it may harm your defence if you do not mention now something which you later rely on in court. Anything you do say may be given in evidence.

B You do not have to say anything. But it may harm your defence if you do not mention when questioned something which you later rely on in court. Anything you do say may be given in evidence.

C You do not have to say anything, but anything you do say may be given in evidence.

D You do not have to say anything, but anything you do say will be noted down, and may be given in evidence.

Question 8.23

KENWRIGHT was arrested and taken to the custody office of a designated police station. The arresting officer told the custody officer that KENWRIGHT had a warning signal on the Police National Computer (PNC) that, while in custody previously, she had concealed razor blades in her mouth and had used them to cause injury to herself. The custody officer decided that KENWRIGHT's mouth should be searched for objects which she might use to harm herself.

Which of the following is true in relation to the search?

A The custody officer can authorise this search at the custody office.

B Only a superintendent can authorise this search at the custody office.

C An inspector can authorise this search at medical premises.

D Only a superintendent can authorise this search at medical premises.

Question 8.24

GOODEY was arrested for deception and was accompanied at the time by her boyfriend, BEDFORD. When he was interviewed at the station, BEDFORD admitted that GOODEY was in possession of a stolen credit card, which she had concealed in her vagina. GOODEY admitted possession of the credit card, but refused to submit to a search.

Could GOODEY be subjected to an 'intimate search' in these circumstances?

A Yes, but this could not be done by force.

B Yes, she is in possession of stolen property.

C Yes, and this may be done, if necessary, by force.

D No, an intimate search may not be authorised in these circumstances.

Question 8.25

In relation to the treatment and welfare of a detained person, the PACE Codes of Practice, Code C, para. 8.6 describes how many meals a detainee should be offered while in custody.

How many meals should be offered to a detained person in any period of 24 hours?

A At least one light meal and at least two main meals.

B At least one light meal and at least one main meal.

C At least two light meals and at least one main meal.

D At least two light meals and at least two main meals.

Question 8.26

JOHNSON is employed as a civilian detention officer by his local police authority.

In relation to duties that he can perform, which of the following is correct?

A He may take a non-intimate sample, but he may not use force to do so.

B He may take a non-intimate sample and may use force to do so where necessary.

C He may take fingerprints and photographs, but may not take non-intimate samples.

D He may take photographs, but may not take fingerprints or non-intimate samples.

Question 8.27

PATCH, aged 21, was arrested for theft and taken to the custody office, where she asked for her father to be informed of her detention. When the custody officer spoke to PATCH's father, he informed her that PATCH was suffering from a mental disorder, which would make it difficult for her to understand questions being put to her about the offence. PATCH's condition was not apparent to either the custody officer or the arresting officer.

In relation to PATCH's detention, what action should the custody officer now take?

A The custody officer must contact an appropriate adult, based on the information received from PATCH's father.

B The custody officer must contact a medical practitioner to seek advice on PATCH's condition before she is interviewed.

C The custody officer may decide whether or not an appropriate adult should be called, based on her own observations.

D The custody officer must contact a medical practitioner or a social worker to seek advice on PATCH's condition before she is interviewed.

Question 8.28

MELFORD has been arrested for an offence of assault and has been given his rights under PACE. He has opted to speak with his solicitor on the phone, but wants to do so privately.

In relation to this request, which of the following statements is correct?

A He should be allowed to speak to his solicitor, but in private only if this is practicable.

B He should be allowed to speak to his solicitor privately, and such a facility should normally be provided.

C He is allowed to consult with his solicitor privately only if this is done in person.

D He should be allowed to consult with his solicitor, but this must be done whilst the custody officer can hear the conversation.

Question 8.29

HURTY was stopped while driving his vehicle on a Saturday morning in Margate. The officer who stopped him, Constable DICKINSON, conducted a Police National Computer (PNC) check and discovered that HURTY was wanted for an offence of burglary in the Newcastle area. Constable DICKINSON arrested HURTY at 10 am and took him to the nearest designated station in Margate, where they arrived at 10.30 am. Constable DICKINSON contacted the police in Newcastle; however, they had no officers available to attend until later that day. The escorting officers finally arrived in the early hours of the next morning, and left with HURTY at 4 am on the Sunday. They transported HURTY to Newcastle, arriving in that force area at 11.10 am; they eventually arrived at Newcastle Police Station at 11.30 am on the Sunday.

What would HURTY's 'relevant time' be, in relation to his detention in Newcastle, if he was not interviewed for the offence in Margate?

A 10.30 am on the Saturday.
B 10 am on the Sunday.
C 11.10 am on the Sunday.
D 11.30 am on the Sunday.

Question 8.30

Constable MOLE arrested WOOD at 3 pm on a Saturday for an offence of theft. Constable MOLE radioed through to her station, but discovered that the custody office could not accept her prisoner at that time, as they were too busy. She decided to utilise her powers under s. 30A of the Police and Criminal Evidence Act 1984, to bail WOOD to the police station the next day. WOOD was released on bail by the officer at 3.30 pm on the Saturday. WOOD was due to answer bail at 2 pm on the Sunday, but he was late and arrived there at 2.30 pm. His detention was authorised by the custody officer at 2.50 pm.

From which time on the Sunday would WOOD's 'relevant time' be calculated, under s. 41 of the Police and Criminal Evidence Act 1984?

A 2.50 pm, the time he appeared before the custody officer on the Sunday.
B 2.20 pm, taking into account the time he was detained by the officer the previous day.
C 2.30 pm, the time he arrived at the police station on the Sunday.
D 2 pm, the time he was due to answer bail on the Sunday.

Question 8.31

MORRISON was arrested for shoplifting and taken to the custody office. On MORRISON's arrival, the custody officer noticed that he was intoxicated. MORRISON was detained for interview and placed in a cell to allow him time to sober up. While he was asleep, MORRISON's sister contacted the custody officer to advise that MORRISON was an alcoholic and might get the shakes while in custody. When he was sober, MORRISON was interviewed and returned to his cell pending preparation of charges. He displayed no symptoms of the shakes, and did not complain of an illness. Unfortunately, while he was in his cell, MORRISON died from asphyxiation. MORRISON was not medically examined while in custody.

Would the police have any liability in relation to the custody officer's failure to act on the information given by MORRISON's sister, and not arranging for him to be medically examined?

A No, as MORRISON's sister is not a registered health care professional or doctor.

B Yes, a custody officer should act on any information relating to a detainee's health care, no matter what the source.

C No, since MORRISON displayed no symptoms of his illness and did not ask to see a doctor.

D Yes, but only if MORRISON's sister informed the custody officer that he was taking medication or seeking medical help for his condition.

Question 8.32

Code C, para. 2.1A of the PACE Codes of Practice defines when a detained person will be deemed to be 'at a police station' for the purposes of detention.

Which of the following statements most accurately describes when a detained person will be 'at a police station' according to this code of practice?

A When the person first arrives within the confines of the custody office, whether or not the custody officer is ready to receive them.

B When the person is first brought before the custody officer, within the confines of the custody office.

C When the person first arrives inside a police station, whether this is the custody office or another part of the building.

D When the person first arrives within the confines of the police station, whether this is inside the building or in an enclosed yard which is part of the police station.

Question 8.33

BRAITHWAITE is 13 years of age and was arrested for an offence of aggravated vehicle taking. On his arrival at the custody office, BRAITHWAITE declined legal advice and stated that neither of his parents would attend the police station to act as an appropriate adult. BOYCE works for the local Youth Offending Team (YOT) and attended to act as appropriate adult. On arrival at the custody office, BOYCE told the custody officer that it was their policy that all juveniles represented by the YOT must also be represented by a solicitor. BOYCE insisted on a solicitor being called.

Would BOYCE be able to overrule BRAITHWAITE's decision, and ensure that he seeks legal advice?

A Yes, as BOYCE was acting in BRAITHWAITE's best interests.

B No, BOYCE had no right to ask for a solicitor to attend once BRAITHWAITE had declined legal advice.

C Yes, because BRAITHWAITE is under 14 and it is in his best interests.

D No, the decision remains with BRAITHWAITE, who does not have to speak to the solicitor.

Question 8.34

Code C, para. 3.4 of the PACE Codes of Practice requires the custody officer to note on the custody record any comment the detainee makes in relation to the arresting officer's account.

According to this code of practice, which of the following statements is correct in relation to who may give the account of the arrest?

A The account may only be given by the arresting officer, but this may be done from a remote location.

B The account may be given from a remote location by the arresting officer, or through another officer accompanying the detainee.

C The arresting officer must be present to give the account in order for any comments to be admissible.

D The officer giving the account must be at the custody office, whether it is the arresting officer or another officer.

Question 8.35

A person may be detained without charge when he/she is suspected of having committed an offence under the Terrorism Act 2000.

What is the maximum period he/she may be detained for?

A 96 hours.

B seven days.

C 14 days.

D 28 days.

Question 8.36

DAWLISH has been interviewed about a large-scale fraud offence. The officers have concluded their investigation but ask that DAWLISH be bailed without charge for further consultation with the National Fraud Office to take place. The officers intend seeking CPS advice on charging when DAWLISH returns on bail. The custody officer is going to release DAWLISH on bail under s. 37(7)(b) of the Police and Criminal Evidence Act 1984 as she believes there is sufficient evidence to charge DAWLISH but is releasing him to allow for further inquiries to be made. The investigating officers, however, are concerned DAWLISH may try to leave the country and ask that as a condition of bail he surrenders his passport.

In relation to this request which of the following is correct?

A The custody officer can impose bail conditions as s. 47 of the Police and Criminal Evidence Act 1984 allows normal powers to impose conditions of bail where a custody officer releases a person on bail under s. 37.

B The custody officer can impose bail conditions as s. 47 of the Police and Criminal Evidence Act 1984 allows normal powers to impose conditions of bail where a custody officer releases a person on bail under s. 37 and CPS advice will be sought when bail is answered.

C The custody officer cannot impose conditions of bail where the custody officer considers that there is sufficient evidence to charge.

D The custody officer cannot impose conditions of bail where a person is released under s. 37 unless the person is released for the purpose of a CPS referral.

Question 8.37

BAILLON has been arrested for an offence of kidnapping and the relevant time began at 10 am on Tuesday. Unfortunately he became ill and had to go to hospital; he left the custody unit at 4 pm arriving at the hospital at 4.30 pm. He remained at the hospital until 9.30 pm and arrived back in custody at 10 pm. Throughout his time in hospital officers remained with him hoping to interview him regarding the whereabouts of the yet unfound victim. However, the casualty doctors refused to allow any questioning of BAILLON.

At what time will BAILLON's detention time end (assuming no extensions are applied for or granted)?

A 10 am on Wednesday; the hospital time counts as officers were present intending to interview BAILLON.

B 3 pm on Wednesday; standard detention time excluding the time spent in hospital.

C 3.30 pm on Wednesday; standard detention time excluding the time spent in hospital and travelling to hospital.

D 4 pm on Wednesday; standard detention time excluding the time spent in hospital and time travelling to and from hospital.

Question 8.38

Constable CHAN is interviewing a 17-year-old person and an appropriate adult has been called. Whilst speaking to the appropriate adult the officer suspects that they have a hearing defect and cannot hear what is being said. The adult makes no mention of this and is happy to be present during the interview.

In these circumstances what action should the officer take?

A The officer should ask an interpreter to sit in at the interview.

B The officer should ask the adult if they want an interpreter and act on their verbal reply.

C The officer should ask an interpreter to sit in at the interview and make a contemporaneous written record of the interview.

D The officer need take no action as the suspect is 17 years of age and therefore does not require an appropriate adult.

Question 8.39

NORMAN is in custody for an offence. She requested legal advice and was allowed to consult on the telephone with the duty solicitor. Shortly afterwards, another solicitor, GULLIVER, summoned by NORMAN's father, attended at the police station.

In relation to GULLIVER, which of the following is correct?

A GULLIVER must be allowed a private consultation with NORMAN.

B NORMAN does not need to be told about GULLIVER as she has already received legal advice.

C NORMAN must be told that GULLIVER is present and should be allowed a consultation.

D NORMAN does not need to be told about GULLIVER as she did not request advice from him.

Question 8.40

Constable DAWSON is interviewing a foreign national and has an interpreter present. The suspect has expressly wished to make a statement under caution in accordance with PACE Code C, Note 12A.

How should this statement be recorded?

A The suspect must record it and the interpreter prepare a translation of it; the suspect shall then sign both statements.

B The interpreter will record the statement in the language in which it is made and then shall sign it themselves; a translation will be made in due course.

C The interpreter will record the statement in the language in which it is made and the suspect shall sign it.

D The interpreter will record the statement in the language in which it is made and the suspect shall sign it; the interpreter shall then immediately provide a translation.

Question 8.41

A suspect fell from a roof during a burglary and was arrested but had to be taken to hospital. The officers fear for the safety of another person still missing and wish to interview the suspect.

In relation to this which of the following is correct?

A They cannot interview the suspect while he/she is a patient in hospital.

B They can interview the suspect with the agreement of a responsible doctor.

C They can interview the suspect only with the agreement of the doctor in charge of the suspect's care.

D They can interview the suspect with the agreement of the doctor in charge of the suspect's care and the custody officer at the nearest designated station.

Question 8.42

The Police and Criminal Evidence Act 1984, Code C, para. 13.4 gives guidance in relation to written statements under caution from suspects, when the statement is made in a language other than English, and an interpreter is present.

What does this code of practice state in relation to who should write the statement under caution?

A The interpreter should write the statement in the language in which it is made, and translate it there and then.

B The interviewee should write it in his or her own language, and the interpreter should translate it there and then.

C The interpreter should write the statement in the language in which it is made, and translate it in due course.

D The interviewee should write it in his or her own language, and the interpreter should translate it in due course.

Question 8.43

O'SULLIVAN was in detention, having been arrested for burglary. Two people escaped from the police at the scene with the stolen property. When O'SULLIVAN's detention was first authorised, he declined legal advice. Constable GOODE, the investigating officer, wished to interview O'SULLIVAN straight away because of the outstanding property and to establish who had been with O'SULLIVAN. However, it was discovered that O'SULLIVAN had injured his leg and the custody officer determined he had to go to hospital after detention was authorised. The custody officer agreed that Constable GOODE could accompany O'SULLIVAN to hospital and interview him there. It transpired that O'SULLIVAN was cooperative and the officer asked him some questions in the ambulance and further questions at the hospital with permission from a doctor.

Assuming that Constable GOODE followed the codes of practice relating to cautioning suspects and legal advice prior to the interviews, how much time will count towards O'SULLIVAN's overall detention time when he returns to the custody office?

A The whole time spent away from the custody office.

B The whole time spent at the hospital.

C Only the time spent during the interview at the hospital.

D Only the time spent questioning him.

Question 8.44

In certain circumstances, Code C, para. 6.9 of the PACE Codes of Practice allows the removal of a legal representative from an interview because of their behaviour.

Which of the following statements is correct in relation to the authorisation required to implement para. 6.9?

A A superintendent may make such an authorisation, but if one is not available, it may be done by an inspector.

B Only an inspector or above may make such an authorisation.

C Either a superintendent or an inspector or above may make an authorisation, but only if they witness the behaviour.

D Only a superintendent or above may make such an authorisation.

Question 8.45

PRIOR works for a firm of solicitors as an accredited representative and attended the custody police station one day on behalf of the firm of solicitors he had recently joined. The custody officer, Sergeant BRADBURY, met PRIOR in the foyer. Unfortunately for PRIOR, Sergeant BRADBURY had just been promoted from a different force area and recognised PRIOR as a person who had been recently arrested and convicted in that area for an offence of burglary, under a different name. When challenged, PRIOR admitted that this was true, and the custody officer contacted the duty inspector.

In these circumstances, could the inspector prevent PRIOR from entering the custody office?

A No, the decision must be made by a superintendent, who must inform the Law Society if entry is refused.

B Yes, and the inspector should inform other custody staff in the area, to ensure that PRIOR is not allowed entry to those either.

C Yes, and the inspector must inform a superintendent, who must inform the Law Society if entry is refused.

D Yes, and the inspector may inform a superintendent, who may inform the Law Society if entry is refused.

Question 8.46

CALLARD has been arrested and is about to be interviewed on audio. Initially CALLARD stated that he did not want a solicitor and the interview commenced. As the officer commences the interview and reminds him of his right to legal advice, CALLARD indicates that he would like legal advice and asks what will happen. The officer says the interview will stop and a solicitor will be called. CALLARD indicates that he does not want to go back in a cell and says he wants to be interviewed now and not wait and does not want a solicitor.

In the circumstances outlined in the scenario, can the audio-recorded interview proceed?

A Yes, provided an officer of the rank of inspector or above has given agreement for the interview to proceed in these circumstances.

B Yes, provided an officer of the rank of inspector has given agreement and the suspect agrees in writing.

C No, as CALLARD has stated that he has changed his mind over legal advice during the interview his solicitor must be contacted.

D No, CALLARD changed his mind due to what the officer said, in these circumstances a solicitor must be called.

ANSWERS

Answer 8.1

Answer **D** — Section 36 of the Police and Criminal Evidence Act 1984 requires that one or more custody officers must be appointed for each designated police station. However, in *Vince* v *Chief Constable of Dorset* [1993] 1 WLR 415 it was held that a chief constable was under a duty to appoint one custody officer for each designated police station and had a discretionary power to appoint more than one but this duty did not go so far as to require a sufficient number to ensure that the functions of custody officer were always performed by them.

The provision of the facility of a custody officer must be reasonable. Section 36(3) states that a custody officer must be an officer of at least the rank of sergeant. However, s. 36(4) allows officers of *any* rank to perform the functions of custody officer at a designated police station if a sergeant is not readily available to perform; answer A is therefore incorrect. This means that, as unlikely as it seems, officers higher in rank than a sergeant can perform custody duties and not just constables; answer B is therefore incorrect. However, this is only where a sergeant is not readily available to perform them; answer C is therefore incorrect.

The effect of s. 36(3) and (4) is that the practice of allowing officers of any other rank to perform the role of custody officer where a sergeant (who has no other role to perform) is in the police station must therefore be unlawful.

Evidence and Procedure, para. 2.8.2

Answer 8.2

Answer **C** — Code C, para. 2.7 states:

> The fact and time of any detainee's refusal to sign a custody record, when asked in accordance with this Code, must be recorded.

There is nothing mentioned about a reason for that refusal; answers A, B and D are therefore incorrect.

Evidence and Procedure, para. 2.8.6

Answer 8.3

Answer **C** — Section 30 of the Police and Criminal Evidence Act 1984 states that an arrested person should be taken to a designated station as soon as practicable after arrest, unless he or she has been bailed prior to arrival at the police station. Section 30A of the Police and Criminal Evidence Act 1984 allows a constable to release on bail a person who is under arrest. However, an arrested person may be dealt with at a non-designated station, provided the person is not likely to be detained for longer than six hours. Answer D is therefore incorrect.

Where a person is taken to a non-designated station, s. 36(7) states that an officer of any rank not involved in the investigation should perform the role of custody officer. However, if no such person is at the station, the arresting officer (or any other officer involved in the investigation) may act as custody officer. Answer B is therefore incorrect.

Where a person is dealt with in a non-designated station in the circumstances described, an officer of at least the rank of inspector at a *designated station* must be informed. Answer A is therefore incorrect.

Evidence and Procedure, para. 2.8.4

Answer 8.4

Answer **B** — The relevant time is the time the person arrives at the police station, or 24 hours after arrest (whichever is earlier). So normally speaking the person in this case should be released by 3.30 pm on Tuesday.

Previously where a case is referred to the Crown Prosecution Service to determine whether proceedings should be instituted (and if so on which charge), it was the case that if the decision to charge was not made at the time, the detained person had to be released on police bail with or without conditions, however, the Police and Justice Act 2006 has amended PACE, s. 37 and the person can now be kept in police detention pending the decision; answer A is therefore incorrect.

However, this change is still subject to the normal time limits for detention, and the person will still have to be released by 3.30 pm on Tuesday; answers C and D are therefore incorrect.

Evidence and Procedure, para. 2.8.16.1

Answer 8.5

Answer **D** — A person in police detention is entitled to have one friend or relative or person known to him/her or who is likely to take an interest in his/her welfare informed of his or her whereabouts as soon as practicable (PACE Code C, para. 5.1); answer C is therefore incorrect.

Code C, paras 3.1 and 5.3 outline that this is a continuing right that applies every time a person is brought to a police station under arrest. This means that a person may have another person (or the same person) informed of his or her detention at the second station; answer A is therefore incorrect. Note it is the detained person's right; no one has the right to be told of detention without the detained person's permission; answer B is therefore incorrect.

Evidence and Procedure, para. 2.8.9

Answer 8.6

Answer **A** — Any person arrested and held in custody at a police station or other premises may, on request, have one person known to them or likely to take an interest in their welfare informed at public expense of their whereabouts as soon as practicable. If the person cannot be contacted the detainee may choose up to two alternatives. If they cannot be contacted, the person in charge of detention or the investigation has discretion to allow further attempts until the information has been conveyed.

So on the fourth alternative contact it is at the discretion of the custody officer not mandated; answer B is therefore incorrect.

There are two alternatives, not three but the custody officer can allow as many as they like; answers C and D are therefore incorrect.

Evidence and Procedure, para. 2.8.9

Answer 8.7

Answer **A** — Section 56 of the Police and Criminal Evidence Act 1984 provides that a person arrested and held in custody at a police station or other premises may, on request, have one friend or relative or person known to him/her or who is likely to take an interest in his/her welfare, informed at public expense of his/her whereabouts as soon as practicable (PACE Code C, para. 5.1). This right can only be delayed if the offence is 'an indictable offence' and an officer of the rank of inspector or above (whether or not connected to the investigation) authorises the delay. The delay can only be for a maximum of 36 hours, and this period is calculated from the 'relevant time', that is the time of arrival at the police station, i.e. 8 am. Not the time detention is authorised or the decision made to hold the suspect incommunicado; answers B and C are therefore incorrect. Although time spent in hospital does not count towards detention time, this does not affect the time a person can be held incommunicado which remains at 36 hours from the relevant time; answer D is therefore incorrect.

Evidence and Procedure, paras 2.8.9, 2.8.20

Answer 8.8

Answer **C** — First, the inspector must be satisfied that O'REILLY is in custody for an indictable offence (which is the case in the scenario). Also, the inspector must have reasonable grounds for believing that if O'REILLY were to exercise his right to have someone informed of his arrest, it might alert other people suspected of the offence but not yet arrested.

PACE Code C, Annex B states that the grounds for action under this Annex shall be recorded and the person informed of them as soon as practicable. The authorisation can initially be made orally, either in person or by telephone, but must be recorded in writing as soon as practicable. Answer D is therefore incorrect.

The decision must be recorded in writing *as soon as practicable*; therefore, answer A is incorrect.

The authorising officer for delaying rights under Code C, para. 5 was reduced from superintendent to inspector by virtue of s. 74 of the Criminal Justice and Police Act 2001; therefore answer B is incorrect.

Evidence and Procedure, para. 2.8.20

Answer 8.9

Answer **D** — It is acceptable to change your mind about not having a solicitor present during an interview, but if one arrives whilst being interviewed the relevant legislation is applied again and the suspect must be told immediately (Code C, para. 6.6(d)(v)). As this must be done immediately, answer B is therefore incorrect.

The only exception to this is where Annex B of Code C applies and this right can be delayed for certain reasons; one of those reasons is that other people suspected of having committed an offence but not yet arrested for it could be alerted; answer A is therefore incorrect.

The initial change of mind about the right would be authorised by an inspector, but any delay in the right once the solicitor arrives must be authorised by a superintendent; answer C is therefore incorrect.

Evidence and Procedure, paras 2.8.10, 2.8.20

Answer 8.10

Answer **D** — Under s. 41(2) of the Police and Criminal Evidence Act 1984, a person's 'relevant time' is calculated from the time he or she arrives at the police station, or 24 hours after he or she was arrested, whichever is earlier. Since most detainees arrive at the station well within 24 hours, their relevant time is generally when they first arrive at the station.

There are several variations contained within s. 41 of the 1984 Act, and the circumstances covered in the question are to be found in s. 41(5). Section 41 states:

(5) If—
  (a) a person is in police detention in a police area in England and Wales ('the first area'); and
  (b) his arrest for an offence is sought in some other police area in England and Wales ('the second area'); and
  (c) he is taken to the second area for the purposes of investigating that offence, without being questioned in the first area in order to obtain evidence in relation to it,
  the relevant time shall be—
  (i) the time 24 hours after he leaves the place where he is detained in the first area; *or*
  (ii) the time at which he arrives at the first police station to which he is taken in the second area,
  whichever is the earlier.

Note that under s. 41(5), the detainee has, in effect, two detention clocks running. It is important to note that the second clock will start earlier if the detained person is questioned about the offence under investigation in the other police area. However, in the scenario PRINCE was *not* questioned about the offence in the first station, and she arrived at the second station *less than 24 hours* after her departure from the first station. Her relevant time is, therefore, her time of arrival at the second station (i.e. 4.30 pm). Answers A, B and C are therefore incorrect.

Evidence and Procedure, para. 2.8.16.1

Answer 8.11

Answer **C** — Under the PACE Codes of Practice before deciding whether to authorise continued detention the officer responsible for the review shall give an opportunity to make representations about the detention to:

(a) the detainee, unless in the case of a review the detainee is asleep;
(b) the detainee's solicitor if available at the time; and
(c) the appropriate adult if available at the time.

Other people having an interest in the detainee's welfare may also make representations at the authorising officer's discretion.

The representations may be made orally in person or by telephone or in writing. The authorising officer may, however, refuse to hear oral representations from the detainee if the officer considers them unfit to make representations because of their condition or behaviour; answers A and B are therefore incorrect.

Should this happen there is no need to ensure another person makes representations; answer D is therefore incorrect.

Evidence and Procedure, para. 2.8.16

Answer 8.12

Answer **D** — Under PACE Code C, para. 3.23, a custody officer should record the grounds for detention in the person's presence if it is practicable to do so. Therefore, in cases such as when a person is drunk or violent, it may not be practicable to record the grounds in his or her presence. Answer B is therefore incorrect. This recording of the grounds must, by virtue of Code C, para. 3.4, be before that person is questioned about any offence; answer C is therefore incorrect.

Answer A is incorrect because if a person cannot understand what is being said, it may be 'impracticable' to record the grounds for detention in his or her presence; however, it is not written as such in the Codes of Practice.

Evidence and Procedure, para. 2.8.7

Answer 8.13

Answer **A** — If the custody officer has determined there is insufficient evidence to charge, the person must be released unless the custody officer has *reasonable grounds for believing* that the person's detention is necessary to preserve or to obtain evidence by questioning the person (s. 37 of the Police and Criminal Evidence Act 1984).

Answer C is incorrect as 'reasonable grounds for believing' requires a greater amount of evidence than 'reasonable cause to suspect'.

Although the person may ultimately be detained until all the suspects are interviewed in these circumstances, each case must be considered on its own merit, against the previous criteria. Answer D is therefore incorrect.

Where the suspicion rests with several suspects, it may be appropriate to hold all suspects until they are all interviewed before deciding whether there is sufficient evidence to warrant a charge against any or all of them. This continues provided suspicion on that individual has not been dispelled in the interim and the questioning is not unnecessarily delayed (*Clarke* v *Chief Constable of North Wales*, Independent, 22 May 2000); answer B is therefore incorrect.

Evidence and Procedure, para. 2.8.17.4

Answer 8.14

Answer **C** — The 'relevant time' is worked out according to the relevant circumstances.

Where a person is arrested and bailed at a place other than a police station the time of arrival at the police station to which the notice of bail states he or she must attend is the relevant time. In this particular case then the relevant time is 6.45 pm, no account is taken of the time they are bailed, or the time they arrived at the wrong police station (irrespective of the fact it is in the same police area); answers A and B are therefore incorrect.

The time of detention relates to the review clock, not the 'relevant time'; answer D is therefore incorrect.

Evidence and Procedure, para. 2.8.16.1

Answer 8.15

Answer **D** — An officer of at least the rank of superintendent can authorise a person's continued detention, beyond 24 hours, up to a maximum of 36 hours. The period can be shorter, but if a shorter period is granted, this can be extended up to the 36-hour limit.

The superintendent must be satisfied that an offence being investigated is an 'indictable offence' and that there is not sufficient evidence to charge, *and* the investigation is being conducted diligently and expeditiously, *and* that the person's detention is necessary to secure and preserve evidence or obtain evidence by questioning (s. 42 of the Police and Criminal Evidence Act 1984).

The extension of a person's detention must be made *within 24 hours* of the relevant time. Also, the extension cannot be granted before *at least two reviews* have been carried out by the reviewing inspector.

Although reviews are normally carried out after six and nine hours, they can be conducted earlier. Section 42(4) is deliberately worded so that the focus is not on the length of time a person has been in custody, but on how many reviews have been conducted.

A superintendent could authorise an extension in these circumstances, but would have to wait until a second review had been conducted.

As STIRLING was arrested for a summary offence, no extension beyond the 24-hour period of initial detention can be made; answers A, B and C are therefore incorrect.

Evidence and Procedure, para. 2.8.16.6

Answer 8.16

Answer **D** — A superintendent may authorise a person's detention without charge for a maximum of 36 hours (s. 42 of the Police and Criminal Evidence Act 1984). Any further periods of detention must be authorised by a magistrate.

A magistrate may initially authorise detention for 36 hours (s. 43). However, this period may be extended by 24 hours upon further application (s. 44), which means that a magistrate may authorise a maximum detention period of 60 hours. A person may not be detained for longer than 96 hours in total without being charged or released. Answers A, B and C are therefore incorrect.

Evidence and Procedure, para. 2.8.16.8

Answer 8.17

Answer **A** — Where a person is in custody for an offence under the Terrorism Act 2000, the first review should be conducted as soon as reasonably practicable after his or her arrest and then at least every 12 hours; after 24 hours it must be conducted by an officer of the rank of superintendent or above. Once a warrant of further detention has been obtained there is no requirement to conduct further reviews. Section 14 of Code H of the Police and Criminal Evidence Act 1984 Codes of Practice provides guidance on terrorism reviews and extensions of detention.

Answer D would be correct only if the person was in custody prior to going to court for the warrant of further detention hearing. Answer B would be incorrect in any circumstances; once a person has been in custody for longer than 24 hours, having been arrested under the 2000 Act, his or her detention must be reviewed by a superintendent. Answer C is incorrect as reviews of people detained under the 2000 Act must be conducted every 12 hours, following the first review.

Evidence and Procedure, para. 2.8.16.13

Answer 8.18

Answer **B** — When a person is arrested under the provisions of the Criminal Justice Act 2003, which allow a person to be re-tried after being acquitted of a serious offence which is a qualifying offence specified in sch. 5 to that Act and not precluded from further prosecution by virtue of s. 75(3) of that Act, the detention provisions of PACE are modified and make an officer of the rank of superintendent or above who has not been directly involved in the investigation responsible for determining whether the evidence is sufficient to charge; answers A, C and D are therefore incorrect.

Evidence and Procedure, para. 2.8.17.2

Answer 8.19

Answer **D** — Under s. 42(1) of the Police and Criminal Evidence Act 1984, detention can only be authorised beyond 24 hours and up to a maximum of 36 hours from the relevant time if:

- an offence being investigated is an 'indictable offence'; and
- an officer of the rank of superintendent or above who is responsible for the station at which the person is detained (referred to here as the authorising officer); and
- that senior officer is satisfied that:
  - there is not sufficient evidence to charge; and
  - the investigation is being conducted diligently and expeditiously; and
  - the person's detention is necessary to secure or preserve evidence relating to the offence or to obtain such evidence by questioning that person.

The grounds for this continuing detention are the same as those when the custody officer made the initial decision to detain, with the additional requirements that the case has been conducted diligently and expeditiously. It is suggested that Art. 5 of the European Convention requires this to be a consideration at all times of detention as a person's right to freedom is one of his or her human rights and any unnecessary periods of detention might be considered actionable. To be able to satisfy the senior officer of this, it will be necessary for the custody record to be available for inspection and details of what inquiries have been made, and evidence that the investigation has been moving at a pace that will satisfy the senior officer that the inquiries should not already have been completed. Code C, para. 15.2A outlines issues to be considered before extending the period of juveniles and mentally vulnerable persons.

The authorising officer (which here must be an officer of the rank of superintendent or above who is responsible for the station at which the person is detained) can authorise detention up to a maximum of 36 hours from the 'relevant time' of detention. The period can be shorter than this and can then be further authorised by that officer or any other officer of the rank of superintendent or above who is responsible for the station at which the person is detained to allow the period to be further extended up to the maximum 36-hour period (s. 42(2)). Code C, Note 15E gives guidance as to which officers this would include. This section outlines that the officer responsible for the station holding the detainee includes a superintendent or above who, in accordance with his/her force operational policy or police regulations, is given that responsibility on a temporary basis whilst the appointed long-term holder is off duty or otherwise unavailable. So although the superintendent in charge of the city centre police station is clearly the person defined by this section, Note 15E allows for eventualities where he or she is absent. It would be wrong to bring forward reviews and authorise extensions some time before the clock runs out to accommodate someone going on leave; answers A and B are therefore incorrect.

The extension of a person's detention by a superintendent or above must be made within 24 hours of the relevant time and cannot be made before at least two reviews have been carried out by a review officer under s. 40 of the 1984 Act (i.e. those normally carried out by an inspector) (s. 42(4)) (Code C, para. 15.2); answer C is therefore incorrect.

Evidence and Procedure, para. 2.8.16.6

Answer 8.20

Answer **D** — While a person is in police detention before charge, his/her detention must be reviewed by an officer of the rank of inspector or above (inspector reviews). This review acts as another safeguard to protect the detained person's right to be detained for only such periods as are necessary to allow for the investigation of an offence. Review officer for the purposes of ss. 40 and 40A of the 1984 Act means, in the case of a person arrested but not charged, an officer of at least inspector rank not directly involved in the investigation and, if a person has been arrested and charged, the custody officer.

The detention of persons in police custody not subject to the statutory review should still be reviewed periodically as a matter of good practice. The purpose of such reviews is to check that the particular power under which a detainee is held continues to apply, that any associated conditions are complied with and to make sure that appropriate action is taken to deal with any changes. This includes the detainee's prompt release when the power no longer applies, or his/her transfer if the power requires the detainee to be taken elsewhere as soon as the necessary arrangements are made. Examples include persons arrested on warrant because they failed to answer bail to appear at court. This review would be carried out by the custody officer not inspector; answers A and C are therefore incorrect, and would be carried out periodically not at set times therefore answer B is incorrect.

Evidence and Procedure, para. 2.8.16.12

Answer 8.21

Answer **B** — Under s. 54(9) of the Police and Criminal Evidence Act 1984, the constable carrying out a search must be of the same sex as the person searched. Section 54 does not prohibit a constable of the opposite sex from being present at a search, provided it is not a strip search or an intimate search. Answer C is therefore incorrect.

Because of the prohibition referred to previously, under s. 54(9), a constable may *not* search a person of the opposite sex, whether during an ordinary search, a strip search or an intimate search. Answers A and D are therefore incorrect.

Evidence and Procedure, para. 2.8.8.1

Answer 8.22

Answer **C** — If a decision is taken to charge the detained person, Code C, para. 16 sets out the procedures to be followed by the custody officer. When a detained person is charged with or informed that he/she may be prosecuted for an offence, para. 16.2 requires him/her to be cautioned. The caution varies slightly from that when arrested or interviewed and is as follows:

> You do not have to say anything. But it may harm your defence if you do not mention now something which you later rely on in court. Anything you do say may be given in evidence.

This caution should not be used in circumstances where the detained person has been denied access to a solicitor in which case the following caution should be used:

> You do not have to say anything, but anything you do say may be given in evidence.

This is answer C; answers A, B and D are therefore incorrect.

Evidence and Procedure, para. 2.8.17

Answer 8.23

Answer **A** — An intimate search may be authorised by an inspector and consists of the physical examination of a person's bodily orifices *other than the mouth*. The physical examination of a person's mouth is *not* classed as an intimate search, and may be authorised by a custody officer for the same reasons as a strip search. Answers B and C are incorrect as the search in the scenario does not amount to an intimate search.

An *intimate search* may be conducted only by a medical practitioner (or registered nurse) at medical premises, where the purpose of the search is to discover a Class A drug. Other *intimate searches* may be conducted at the custody office by police officers (provided all the criteria are met). Answer D is therefore incorrect for this reason.

Evidence and Procedure, para. 2.8.19

Answer 8.24

Answer **D** — An intimate search may be authorised by an inspector and consists of the physical examination of a person's bodily orifices other than the mouth. The search may be authorised *only* when the authorising officer has reasonable grounds for believing that the person has concealed an article which could be used to cause physical injury, or has concealed a Class A drug which he or she intended to supply to another or export.

Since the search may be authorised only for these purposes, answers A, B and C are incorrect. Where an intimate search is authorised correctly, reasonable force may be used (s. 117 of the Police and Criminal Evidence Act 1984). However, in these circumstances, the use of force is not permitted.

Evidence and Procedure, para. 2.8.19

Answer 8.25

Answer **C** — At least *two light meals* and *one main meal* shall be offered in any period of 24 hours. Answers A, B and D are therefore incorrect. Drinks should be provided at meal times and upon reasonable request between meal times (PACE Code C, para. 8.6). Meals should so far as practicable be offered at recognised meal times (Code C, Note 8B).

Evidence and Procedure, para. 2.8.12

Answer 8.26

Answer **B** — Sections 38 and 39 of the Police Reform Act 2002 provide certain police powers for police authority employees. This recognises that many of the functions that were traditionally carried out by police officers are now performed by accredited (and trained) staff, and gives statutory footing to their actions. Part of this group are detention officers, and they are given power to carry out most of the functions that were previously given only to police officers. It includes taking non-intimate samples; answers C and D are therefore incorrect. By virtue of s. 38(8) of the Police Reform Act 2002, detention officers have the same power to use *reasonable* force that is given to police officers in the execution of the same duties; answer A is therefore incorrect.

Evidence and Procedure, para. 2.8.3

Answer 8.27

Answer **A** — Code C, Note 1G defines 'mentally vulnerable' as applying to any detainees who, because of their mental state or capacity, may not understand the significance of what is said, of questions or of their replies. 'Mental disorder' is defined by s. 1(2) of the Mental Health Act 1983 (as amended by s. 1 of the Mental Health Act 2007), as 'any disorder or disability of mind'. Code C, para. 1.4 provides further guidance, if there is any doubt, the detained person should be treated as if they are mentally vulnerable. There is no room for interpretation, and the custody officer must contact an appropriate adult in these circumstances. Answer C is therefore incorrect.

Although a custody officer may contact a medical practitioner or a social worker for advice as to how to deal with a person suffering from a mental disorder, Code C, para. 1.4 makes it clear that the information given by PATCH's father is sufficient to ensure that a person is treated as such in these circumstances. Answers B and D are therefore incorrect.

Evidence and Procedure, para. 2.8.5

Answer 8.28

Answer **B** — Code C, Note 6J clearly outlines that whenever a detainee exercises his or her right to legal advice by consulting with or communicating with a solicitor, he or she must be allowed to do so in private; therefore, answer D is incorrect. This means both personal consultations and those done via the telephone; answer C is therefore incorrect.

Although this may well present practical difficulties in a busy custody unit, Note 6J makes it clear that the normal expectation is that such a facility *will* be available, and a private consultation should be allowed; answer A is therefore incorrect.

Evidence and Procedure, para. 2.8.10

Answer 8.29

Answer **B** — Questions relating to relevant times can appear daunting, but they can be solved using fairly simple constructed formulas. In the scenario, HURTY has not been arrested for a 'local offence' therefore the relevant time is the time he arrived at a police station in the police area where he was wanted (not just the time he arrived in that force's area; therefore answer C is incorrect) *or* 24 hours after arrest, whichever is the earliest. He was arrested at 10 am on Saturday, and arrived at the station at 11.30 am on the Sunday, therefore the relevant time is 10 am on the Sunday (by applying the formula, and noting that 10 am is in fact earlier than 11.30 am!). Answer D is therefore incorrect. Had HURTY been questioned by Margate police about the burglary, the relevant time would have been 10.30 am on the Saturday (time of arrival at local station); but as he was not questioned, answer A is incorrect.

Evidence and Procedure, para. 2.8.16.1

Answer 8.30

Answer **C** — Section 41(2)(ca) of the Police and Criminal Evidence Act 1984 takes into account police officers' powers to bail people from the scene of their arrest. Where a person has been bailed under s. 30A of the Act, his or her relevant time will be the time that he or she arrives at the station (2.30 pm in the scenario). Answers A, B and D are incorrect for this reason.

Evidence and Procedure, para. 2.8.16.1

Answer 8.31

Answer **B** — Any information that is available about the detained person should be considered in deciding whether to request a medical examination. In *R v HM Coroner for Coventry, ex parte Chief Constable of Staffordshire Police* [2000] 164 JP 665 the detained person had been drunk on arrest and was detained to be interviewed. The detained person made no complaint of his condition but his sister called the police to advise them that he would get the shakes. It was clear at interview and the following morning that he did have the shakes but no complaint was made and no doctor was called. A verdict of accidental death aggravated by neglect was an option in the case, as the deceased had died while in police custody. The court considered the facts, such as the deceased's withdrawal and the warning as to his condition, from which a properly directed jury could have concluded that had certain steps been taken it was at least possible that the deceased would not have died. In this case a verdict of accidental death aggravated by neglect was left open to the jury, even though a doctor at the inquest gave evidence that he doubted whether calling a doctor would have made any difference to the eventual outcome.

The clear message from this case is that the custody officer must take into account *any* information about a person's health, whether it comes from the detainee, the arresting officer or any other source. Answer A is therefore incorrect. Whether or not the detainee displayed symptoms of illness is immaterial and therefore answer C is incorrect. Also, the fact that the detainee's sister failed to mention whether or not the person was taking medication or seeking medical help is also immaterial and answer D is therefore incorrect.

Evidence and Procedure, para. 2.8.13.1

Answer 8.32

Answer **D** — According to the PACE Codes of Practice, Code C, para. 2.1A:

> A person is deemed to be 'at a police station' for these purposes if they are within the boundary of any building or enclosed yard which forms part of that police station.

This definition is far wider than merely inside a police station (and answer C is therefore incorrect) or within the confines of a custody office (and answer B is incorrect). It is important to note this addition to the Codes of Practice, because the time the person arrives at the police station forms the basis of a detainee's relevant time and could have an effect later in the person's detention when investigating officers are seeking extensions. It should also be noted that since many custody offices have CCTV cameras fitted, the accuracy of such information is crucial in case of challenges. Answer A is completely wrong, as a person may be waiting in a police vehicle in a yard outside a busy custody office for some time and this will count towards their overall detention time.

Evidence and Procedure, para. 2.8.6

Answer 8.33

Answer **D** — The situation in this question is covered by Code C, para. 6.5A of the PACE Codes of Practice, which states:

In the case of a juvenile, an appropriate adult should consider whether legal advice from a solicitor is required. If the juvenile indicates that they do not want legal advice, the appropriate adult has the right to ask for a solicitor to attend if this would be in the best interests of the person. However, the detained person cannot be forced to see the solicitor if he is adamant that he does not wish to do so.

As can be seen from this paragraph, a juvenile cannot be made to speak with a legal representative, even if this is in his or her best interests, regardless of his or her age or the local YOT's policy. Answers A and C are therefore incorrect. The appropriate adult *does* have the right to ask for a solicitor to attend if it is in the best interests of the detainee (and answer B is therefore incorrect); however, this right does not extend to forcing the juvenile to speak to the solicitor once he/she has arrived at the custody office.

Evidence and Procedure, para. 2.8.10

Answer 8.34

Answer **B** — The PACE Codes of Practice, Code C, para. 3.4 states that the custody officer shall note on the custody record any comment the detainee makes in relation to the arresting officer's account but shall not invite comment. If the arresting officer is not physically present when the detainee is brought to a police station, the arresting officer's account must be made available to the custody officer remotely or by a third party on the arresting officer's behalf. If the custody officer authorises a person's detention, subject to para. 1.8, that officer must record the grounds for detention in the detainee's presence and at the same time, inform them of the grounds. The detainee must be informed of the grounds for their detention before they are questioned about any offence.

Answer A is correct in the sense that the information regarding a person's arrest may be given from a remote location; however, it is incorrect as the information may also be given by another officer accompanying the detainee. Answer C is incorrect, as the arresting officer need not be present when giving the information, and answer D is incorrect as para. 3.4 clearly states that the information may be given from a remote location.

Evidence and Procedure, para. 2.8.7

Answer 8.35

Answer **C** — The maximum period a person may be detained without charge under PACE is 96 hours, following the granting of an extension by the magistrates' court. However, when a person is in police detention and is suspected of having committed an offence under the Terrorism Act 2000, the *maximum* period is 14 days. Answers A, B and D are therefore incorrect.

Evidence and Procedure, para. 2.8.16.3

Answer 8.36

Answer **D** — Where the custody officer considers there is sufficient evidence to charge and the person is bailed after charge or bailed without charge and on bail for the purpose of enabling the CPS to make a decision regarding case disposal, the custody officer may impose conditions on that bail; answer C is therefore incorrect.

Section 47 of the Police and Criminal Evidence Act 1984 states:

(1A) The normal powers to impose conditions of bail shall be available to him where a custody officer releases a person on bail under section 37 above or section 38(1) above (including that subsection as applied by section 40(10) above) but not in any other cases.

However, where a person is bailed under s. 37 for a purpose other than a CPS referral, as is the case in the question scenario, then conditions cannot be applied to that bail; answer A is therefore incorrect.

The bail must be for CPS advice, it is irrelevant that CPS advice will be sought when bail is answered; answer B is therefore incorrect.

Evidence and Procedure, para. 2.8.17.6

Answer 8.37

Answer **D** — The standard detention time is 24 hours from the relevant time, so all things being equal the detention time will end at 10 am Wednesday.

If a detained person is taken to hospital for medical treatment, the time at hospital and the period spent travelling to and from the hospital does not count towards the relevant time unless the person is asked questions for the purpose of obtaining evidence about an offence. This applies only where questions are actually asked not intended; answer A is therefore incorrect. Also note that the clock would effectively be 'off' from the moment travelling to the hospital begins until it ends. In this scenario that is from 4 pm to 10 pm. This is six hours off the clock, effectively six hours added to 10 am, making it 4 pm on Wednesday; answers A, B and C are therefore incorrect.

Where questioning takes place, this period would count towards the relevant time and therefore the custody officer must be informed of it (s. 41(6) PACE).

Evidence and Procedure, para. 2.8.16.1

Answer 8.38

Answer **A** — As a confession can be very damning evidence against a defendant, it is important to provide safeguards that give all suspects the same level of protection. The PACE Codes of Practice recognise certain groups as being in need of additional protection. These groups include young people, people who do not speak English, those suffering from a mental impairment and those who are deaf. Such suspects must not be interviewed without the relevant person being present.

If the suspect appears to be deaf or there is any doubt about his/her hearing or speaking ability, an interpreter should be found (unless he/she agrees in writing to proceed without an interpreter (Code C, para. 13.5)). This requirement also applies in the case of the appropriate adult who appears to be deaf or there is doubt about his/her hearing or speaking ability; as this is a requirement and not an option answer B is incorrect.

If the suspect is deaf or there is doubt about his/her hearing ability, a contemporaneous written record should be made as well as the audio recording, however, this only applies to the suspect and not an appropriate adult; answer C is therefore incorrect. The requirement of Code C, para. 13.5 applies to 17-year-old suspects; answer D is therefore incorrect.

Evidence and Procedure, para. 2.8.14

Answer 8.39

Answer **C** — If a solicitor arrives at the station to see a suspect, the suspect must be asked whether he or she would like to see the solicitor *regardless of what legal advice has already been received* and regardless of whether or not the advice was requested by the suspect; answers B and D are therefore incorrect (PACE Code C, para. 6.15). Note that it is the suspect's choice whether to speak to the solicitor, who has no automatic right of consultation even if summoned by a relative, and answer A is therefore incorrect. However, where a solicitor does arrive at the police station to see a suspect, that suspect has to be told of the solicitor's presence and must be allowed to consult with the solicitor should he or she wish to do so.

Evidence and Procedure, para. 2.8.10

Answer 8.40

Answer **C** — Statements under caution, particularly of a detained person, are less common than interviews. If a person has been interviewed and it has been audio or visually recorded or an interview has been recorded contemporaneously in writing, a statement under caution should normally be conducted only at the person's express wish (Code C, Note 12A).

When completing the statement, the person must always be invited to write down what he/she wants to say and should be allowed to do so without any prompting, except that a police officer may indicate which matters are material or question any ambiguity in the statement. In the case of a person making a statement in a language other than English, Code C, para. 13.4 states:

- (a) the interpreter shall record the statement in the language it is made;
- (b) the person shall be invited to sign it [answer B is therefore incorrect];
- (c) an official English translation shall be made in due course [answer D is therefore incorrect].

(In these cases, para. 13.4 means that the person will not be invited to write the statement him/herself which is an exception to the guidance in Annex D; answer A is therefore incorrect.)

Evidence and Procedure, para. 2.8.14

Answer 8.41

Answer **B** — Note that a person in police detention at a hospital must not be questioned without the agreement of a responsible doctor (Code C, para. 14.2); answer A is therefore incorrect. If a person is questioned in these circumstances, he is entitled to consult a solicitor. The Code does not mention, unlike drink/drive legislation, the doctor in immediate charge of the person's care; answers C and D are therefore incorrect.

Evidence and Procedure, para. 2.8.15

Answer 8.42

Answer **C** — Code C, para. 13.4 states that where a person makes a statement under caution in a language other than English, the interpreter should record the statement in the language in which it is made, the person must be invited to sign it, and an official English translation must be made in due course. There is no provision in the Codes of Practice for the interviewee to write the statement, therefore answers B and D are incorrect. Also, there is no requirement for the statement to be translated immediately, and answer A is therefore incorrect.

Evidence and Procedure, para. 2.8.14

Answer 8.43

Answer **D** — While the situation in the question is unusual, the actions of the police were perfectly legal. Under the PACE Codes of Practice, Code C, para. 14.2, if a person is in police detention at a hospital he/she may not be questioned without the agreement of a responsible doctor. Note 14A continues: 'if questioning takes place at a hospital under paragraph 14.2, or on the way to or from a hospital, *the period of questioning concerned* counts towards the total period of detention permitted' (emphasis added). Answers A and B are therefore incorrect. Answer C is incorrect, because both the interview on the way to the hospital and the interview at the hospital will count towards the overall detention time.

Note that in circumstances where a person is interviewed away from the custody office, it would be advisable as far as possible to record the interview on a portable tape recorder to demonstrate that the Codes of Practice have been complied with. Also, the situation would have been different if the detainee had requested legal advice when detention was first authorised. In this case, permission to interview without the solicitor being present would have to be granted either by a superintendent (if the matter was urgent—Code C, para. 6.6(b)) or by an inspector (if the detainee changed his/her mind—Code C, para. 6.6(d)).

Evidence and Procedure, para. 2.8.15

Answer 8.44

Answer **A** — Provision is made under the PACE Codes of Practice, Code C, para. 6.9 to remove a solicitor from an interview, if the interviewer considers a solicitor is acting in such a way that their conduct is such that the interviewer is unable to put questions to the suspect properly. Further guidance is contained in para. 6.10, which states that the interviewing officer must stop the interview and consult an officer not below superintendent rank, if one is readily available, and otherwise an officer not below inspector rank not connected with the investigation. Since either of these officers may take the decision, answers B and D are incorrect. Note 6E states:

> An officer who takes the decision to exclude a solicitor must be in a position to satisfy the court the decision was properly made. In order to do this they may need to witness what is happening.

It is not mandatory that the authorising officer witnesses the behaviour (therefore answer C is incorrect); however, it would be advisable to do so in order that an informed decision is reached. In practice, it is advised that the authorising officer listens to the audio recording of the interview to assist in the decision-making process. The solicitor could then be given a warning and the interviewing officer advised to stop the interview if it re-occurs. This way, the solicitor will have been given every opportunity to correct his/her behaviour.

Evidence and Procedure, para. 2.8.10

Answer 8.45

Answer **D** — An accredited or probationary representative sent to provide advice by, and on behalf of, a solicitor shall be admitted to the police station for this purpose unless an officer of inspector rank or above considers such a visit will hinder the investigation and directs otherwise (PACE Code C, para. 6.12A). Answer A is therefore incorrect.

The inspector should take into account in particular whether the identity and status of an accredited or probationary representative have been satisfactorily established and/or whether he/she is of suitable character to provide legal advice, e.g. a person with a criminal record is unlikely to be suitable unless the conviction was for a minor offence and not recent (para. 6.13).

The exclusion of an accredited or probationary solicitor has to be considered in relation to the specific investigation and whether that person is likely to interfere with the investigation, and the decision has to be made in relation to each individual case. It is *not* permissible to have blanket bans on such persons. Answer B is therefore incorrect.

In relation to informing the Law Society, if an inspector considers a particular solicitor or firm of solicitors is persistently sending probationary representatives who are unsuited to provide legal advice, he/she should inform an officer of at least superintendent rank, who may wish to take the matter up with the Law Society. This is not mandatory in every case and would depend on the company itself. Answer C is therefore incorrect.

Lastly, if the inspector refuses access to an accredited or probationary representative, the inspector must notify the solicitor's company, to give them an opportunity to make alternative arrangements (para. 6.14).

Evidence and Procedure, para. 2.8.10

Answer 8.46

Answer **B** — The right to legal advice is an absolute right, however, once the initial decision is made by the suspect they may change their mind; if they do, Code C, para. 6.6(d) applies. If a suspect changes their mind, or re-changes it then the auspices of Code C apply again. An interview can go ahead without a solicitor if an inspector speaks to the suspect about their decision and agrees that the reasons outlined are appropriate for the interview to continue but the suspect must agree in writing; answer A is therefore incorrect.

It is immaterial when or how the suspect changes their mind. That is why the inspector will speak to them, to ensure the suspect understands their decision; answers C and D are therefore incorrect.

Evidence and Procedure, para. 2.8.10

9 | Identification

STUDY PREPARATION

The area of identification was regulated by the Police and Criminal Evidence Act 1984 and principally Code D of the Codes of Practice. This is the starting point. However, identification is a very fertile area for defence lawyers and, not surprisingly, case law in this area has extended or restricted the legislation—depending on your viewpoint. One thing is certain—the case law has complicated the subject for those who are trying to study it.

The law regulating the various methods of identification (e.g. witness testimony, ID parades, DNA samples and fingerprints) should be known, and you should be able to recognise the relevant circumstances and authorisation levels that must exist.

QUESTIONS

Question 9.1

Officers in London are investigating a robbery at a bank and have obtained colour CCTV of the robbers leaving the premises. Other officers have been asked to view the CCTV to identify the as yet unknown suspects and Constable DEVONISH has attended to view the CCTV. The officer watches the footage, and during the first showing he fails to recognise anyone. The officer is shown the footage a second time and while watching the footage he says, 'the first one out the door could be Jimmy McGOWAN, as he has a pronounced limp like McGOWAN, he is also wearing a West Ham football scarf to cover his face, and McGOWAN also wears a West Ham scarf all the time, but it might not be him'.

In relation to what the officer says, which of the following is correct in relation to what should be recorded about this identification?

A The only fact that should be recorded is 'it might not be him' as this undermines the identification.

B The only fact that should be recorded is that the officer was shown the footage twice.

C Everything relating to the identification should be recorded, however, the factors that triggered identification need not be recorded.

D Everything relating to the identification should be recorded, including the factors that triggered identification.

Question 9.2

BREWSTER is a witness to an armed robbery and is being interviewed by a police officer. BREWSTER provides a handwritten note that she wrote down of the description of the suspect she had seen commit the robbery. The writing on the note is very clear and outlines in detail the description of the suspect.

In relation to this which of the following is correct?

A The officer should now record that description in her pocket notebook, this will then be a record of that first description.

B The officer should now record that description in the witness's statement, this will then be a record of that first description.

C The officer must ask the witness to time and date and then sign the handwritten note as the first description.

D The officer should retain the handwritten note as this is the first description.

Question 9.3

Constable SWEETING is on patrol when he sees a robbery taking place and chases the suspect on foot. The officer radios a description of the offender including a unique hairstyle. Another officer recognises the suspect from the description of his hair and tells the other officers whom to look out for. Constable SWEETING does not know this person but while driving around he sees the suspect and arrests him for the offence.

In relation to this which of the following is correct?

A As the suspect was known, Constable SWEETING should have been kept apart from the suspect; the identification may be excluded.

B As the suspect was known, Constable SWEETING should have been withdrawn from the area as he may have to take part in an identification process.

C Constable SWEETING does not know the suspect, therefore his arrest of him is not in issue.

D Constable SWEETING should now take part in an identification process to confirm the identity of the suspect.

Question 9.4

Inspector GOULD is carrying out an identification procedure and has a copy of the first description of the suspect as obtained from a witness. The suspect is represented by a solicitor.

What should the Inspector do with this record?

A The Inspector must give it to the solicitor prior to the identification procedure taking place.

B The Inspector must give it to the suspect or his/her solicitor prior to the identification procedure taking place.

C The Inspector must, where practicable, give it only to the solicitor prior to the identification procedure taking place.

D The Inspector must, where practicable, give it to the suspect or his/her solicitor prior to the identification procedure taking place.

Question 9.5

Constable MEMORY was on mobile patrol and was accompanied by a colleague from the Dutch police. While stationary at traffic lights a car pulled alongside them. Constable MEMORY recognised the driver as NANCARROW whom she knew was a disqualified driver. In the vehicle was NANCARROW's wife, whom the officer also recognised. The vehicles were next to each other for no more than 30 seconds, and NANCARROW's vehicle made off and was not traced. NANCARROW was arrested some time later and denied being the driver and demanded an identification parade. The Dutch officer is now with another force several hundred miles away.

In relation to identification procedures which of the following is correct?

A An identification must be held with Constable MEMORY as a witness, it is not practical to hold one for the Dutch officer.

B An identification procedure should be held with the Dutch officer as a witness, there would be no useful purpose in having Constable MEMORY as a witness.

C An identification procedure should be held with both Constable MEMORY and the Dutch officer as witnesses.

D An identification procedure need not be held as it is not practical to hold one for the Dutch officer and there would be no useful purpose in having Constable MEMORY as a witness.

Question 9.6

PRYCE was approached by three men and robbed of his wallet. This was witnessed by someone who observed the suspects at length; the witness could describe the age of the men and the clothes that they were wearing but does not give descriptions of them. Three men are arrested later and the police are considering whether an identification parade should be held with the witness as the men deny being the robbers although they accept they were at the scene when it took place.

In these circumstances should an identification procedure be held?

A Yes, this is an issue of identification and it is disputed; a procedure should be held.

B Yes, even though this is only an issue of participation a procedure should be held.

C No, the men accept they were at the scene so an identification procedure would not be of any assistance.

D No, as this is identification of clothing and not the suspects an identification procedure would not be of any assistance.

Question 9.7

Police officers are dealing with a murder inquiry during which there was significant publicity to identify a suspect. The suspect has been identified and an identification procedure is being considered by the police.

What is the requirement on the police in relation to material released by them to the press for publicity purposes?

A The material need only be retained and disclosed in accordance with the relevant codes of the Criminal Procedure and Investigations Act 1996.

B The material must be shown to either the suspect or his/her solicitor prior to any identification procedure taking place.

C The material must be shown, where practicable, to either the suspect or his/her solicitor prior to any identification procedure taking place.

D The material need not be retained by the police or shown to either the suspect or his/her solicitor as it has already been in the public domain.

Question 9.8

Police are investigating an offence and have obtained a voice recording of the suspect, who they suspect to be BRUSTARD. The victim is his estranged wife and the police are considering playing her the recording to see if she can recognise the voice and if that can be used in evidence.

Which of the following is correct?

A The sample should be of an adequate size to make it attributable to the suspect by the witness.

B The sample should be of an adequate size to make it attributable to the suspect by the witness and any recognition would be stand-alone evidence.

C The sample should be of an adequate size to make it attributable to a single person speaking to ensure identification is robust and any recognition would be stand-alone evidence.

D The sample should be of an adequate size to make it attributable to a single person speaking to ensure identification is robust.

Question 9.9

CURBISHLEY was arrested on suspicion of burglary, as fingerprint identification from the scene of the crime was available. CURBISHLEY initially denied the offence, and the taking of his fingerprints was authorised to prove or disprove his involvement in the offence and taken for that purpose. Following further comparison and further interviews, CURBISHLEY admitted the offence. CURBISHLEY has been charged and the officer in charge of the case wishes to take his fingerprints. CURBISHLEY refuses this request.

Which of the following statements is true?

A As CURBISHLEY has been charged, his fingerprints can be taken without his consent.

B As CURBISHLEY has been charged, his fingerprints can be taken only *with* his consent.

C As CURBISHLEY has refused, an inspector's authority, in writing, is required.

D As CURBISHLEY has refused, an inspector's authority, which can be oral or written, is required.

Question 9.10

GRAVES has been arrested and charged with an offence, he appears at court and is found not guilty. When he was in custody his fingerprints were taken and he is wondering now whether these fingerprints will be destroyed.

In relation to this which of the following is correct?

A As he has been arrested and charged with an offence his fingerprints can be retained for the prevention and detection of crime.

B As he has been found not guilty of the offence he was charged with the fingerprints must be destroyed.

C If he was charged with a qualifying offence his fingerprints will be retained for five years.

D If he was charged with a minor offence then his fingerprints will be deleted.

Question 9.11

HAVARD has been charged with driving while disqualified, and when interviewed he made no comment at all. The police have on record a person with the same name who was also disqualified in the same year that HAVARD is suspected of being disqualified, and identification of HAVARD as the actual disqualified driver has not been made. The Crown Prosecution Service (CPS) propose to call HAVARD's solicitor; in addition to currently representing HAVARD she was present in court when the male known as HAVARD was disqualified. The CPS only intend asking questions for the purpose of solely identifying the person disqualified from driving at the original court hearing.

Can the solicitor be called to identify HAVARD as the disqualified driver?

A The solicitor cannot be called, as this would breach legal professional privilege.

B The solicitor cannot be called, as this would breach HAVARD's right to be represented by a lawyer of his choice.

C The solicitor can be called, as she was a person present when HAVARD was originally disqualified.

D The solicitor should not ordinarily be called, but can be called and this should only be entertained as a last resort.

Question 9.12

GUILLETTE is standing trial for rape, and DNA evidence will be an issue for the jury.

In relation to DNA evidence against GUILLETTE, which of the following is true?

A The DNA evidence will be sufficient to prove GUILLETTE was the assailant.

B The DNA evidence must be supported by other direct evidence.

C The DNA evidence can be supported only by other identification evidence.

D The DNA evidence can be supported by mere circumstantial evidence.

Question 9.13

Section 62 of the Police and Criminal Evidence Act 1984 allows for the taking from a suspect of intimate and non-intimate samples. Police officers wish to take a penile swab from a suspect in custody.

Is this penile swab an intimate sample?

A Yes, this is an intimate sample even though it is not a body orifice.

B Yes, as the legislation states that the penis is in effect a body orifice.

C No, as intimate samples are samples of blood, semen, or any other tissue fluid, urine or pubic hair.

D No, as a non-intimate sample is described as a swab taken from any part of a person's body including the mouth but not any other body orifice.

Question 9.14

McGREGOR is a 16-year-old boy who has been arrested following an allegation of rape against him. When he was brought into custody a member of social services was called to act as appropriate adult, however, they left when the police said the interviews would be held in several hours' time. The officer in charge of the investigation now wants to take an intimate sample which would require the removal of the suspect's clothing. McGREGOR agrees to give the sample and states he does not want the social worker to be present. The social worker is phoned and agrees that she does not need to be present when the juvenile's clothes are removed.

Can the police now lawfully remove the juvenile's clothes to obtain an intimate sample?

A Yes, the suspect has agreed and indicated he does not wish to have an appropriate adult present.

B Yes, the suspect has agreed and indicated he does not wish to have an appropriate adult present, and the appropriate adult agrees.

C No, as the appropriate adult was not present with the juvenile when he elected not to have an appropriate adult present.

D No, as an appropriate adult would have to be present at all times when an intimate sample is taken, provided they are the same sex.

Question 9.15

HIGGINS was arrested for an offence of theft and a mouth swab was taken lawfully from him. He was released from custody and later the sample taken proved to be unsuitable or insufficient.

In relation to obtaining another sample, which of the following is true?

A It must be re-taken within six months of the date of release.

B It must be re-taken within six months of the officer being told it was unsuitable or insufficient.

C It must be re-taken within one year of the date of release.

D It must be re-taken within one year of the officer being told it was unsuitable or insufficient.

Question 9.16

Intimate samples may be taken from persons in police detention or, in certain circumstances, from persons who are not in police detention.

In relation to the authority needed for the taking of such samples, which of the following is true?

A Inspector's authority in detention; superintendent's authority not in detention.

B Inspector's authority irrespective of whether the person is in detention or not.

C Superintendent's authority irrespective of whether the person is in detention or not.

D Superintendent's authority in detention; inspector's authority not in detention.

Question 9.17

WILTORD was arrested by Detective Constable COLE for an assault. He was released on bail for an identification procedure and his fingerprints were taken prior to his release. On the day that he was due to answer bail, WILTORD's brother, who was similar in appearance, attended the station instead of WILTORD, in an attempt to confuse witnesses. However, after the brother had been booked in by the custody officer, Detective Constable COLE suspected that he was not the person who had been released on bail. Detective Constable COLE contacted the duty inspector by telephone and asked for permission to obtain fingerprints from WILTORD's brother because of his suspicions.

Would the duty inspector be able to authorise such a request in these circumstances?

A No, this power is only given to a court, when a person has been charged with an offence.

B No, this power is only given to an inspector where a person has been charged with an offence.

C Yes, but the fingerprints may be taken only when the inspector has provided written authority.

D Yes, and the fingerprints may be taken immediately.

Question 9.18

HOPE was stationary in his car when he was approached by two men who threatened him with knives and stole his wallet. The men did not disguise their appearance and had local accents. Shaken by the experience, HOPE visited his sister who suggested he searched Twitter to see if he recognised anyone. After several days he saw one of the men had an account and had 'tweeted' on the day of the robbery that he had come into some money.

In relation to this identification, which of the following is correct?

A The suspect would now be a known suspect and no further identification procedure should be used.

B This is now a recognition case and no further identification procedure should be used.

C The police should obtain as much evidence as possible to establish how the identification was made using Twitter.

D The police would now have to show photographs to HOPE in controlled conditions following the procedure laid down in Annex E of Code D of PACE.

Question 9.19

Samples can be defined as 'intimate' or 'non-intimate'.

Which of the following will be classed as 'non-intimate' within the definition outlined in Code D, para. 6.1 of the PACE Codes of Practice?

A A skin impression other than a fingerprint.

B A sample of urine.

C A blood sample.

D A dental impression.

Question 9.20

Police officers have arrested TIMSON, who is 12 years of age, for a burglary offence. The officers wish to take a footwear impression as part of their investigation of this offence.

In relation to this which of the following is correct?

A This could only be done with written consent from TIMSON and his parents.

B This could only be done with the written consent of TIMSON's parents.

C This can be done without consent as he has been arrested for a recordable offence.

D This cannot be done as he is under the age of 14 years.

Question 9.21

MURPHY is 16 years of age and in police detention, having been arrested on suspicion of rape. Authorisation has been given to take samples of MURPHY's pubic hair, which will involve the removal of his clothing. MURPHY has agreed to the provision of the samples and has signed the custody record accordingly. MURPHY's mother was at the custody office earlier for the interviews, but has now gone to work. She will not be available to return to the custody office for another three hours.

Would the police need to consult with MURPHY's mother before taking the sample of pubic hairs in these circumstances?

A No, he does not want his mother there and has signed the custody record; this is sufficient.

B Yes, because MURPHY's mother was not present when he made the decision.

C No, because MURPHY's mother has left the station and is not readily available.

D No, because MURPHY is over 14, he may make such a decision for himself.

Question 9.22

Constable CANALE is the first officer to arrive at the scene of a robbery. The officer is given a first description of the suspect by the victim.

How should the officer record this description?

A The officer can only record it in his pocket notebook and it must be in a visible and legible form.

B The officer can only record it in his pocket notebook and in note form provided it will be in a visible and legible form in a s. 9 statement.

C The officer can record it on any paper-based record provided it is in a visible and legible form.

D The officer can record it electronically or on any paper-based record provided it is in a visible and legible form.

Question 9.23

FELICE was arrested for an offence of theft, but will not be charged as there was insufficient evidence. Police wish to take FELICE's photograph for future use while she is still in police detention.

In relation to taking the photograph, which of the following is correct?

A The photograph can be taken without FELICE's consent and used for identification procedures.

B The photograph can be taken, but only if FELICE gives her permission.

C The photograph can be taken without FELICE's consent, but cannot be used for identification procedures.

D The photograph cannot be taken, as FELICE has not been charged or reported for a recordable offence.

Question 9.24

Authorisation to search detainees and examine them to ascertain their identity under s. 54A of the Police and Criminal Evidence Act 1984 must be obtained by the custody officer.

Who, out of the following, can correctly give such authorisation?

A An officer of at least the rank of superintendent only, either orally or in writing, provided it is confirmed in writing as soon as practicable.

B An officer of at least the rank of inspector before charge, or a custody officer after charge, either orally or in writing, provided it is confirmed in writing as soon as practicable.

C An officer of at least the rank of inspector, either orally or in writing, provided it is confirmed in writing as soon as practicable.

D An officer of at least the rank of inspector, and permission may only be given in writing.

Question 9.25

WHITE is 14 years of age and has been arrested on suspicion of raping a girl his own age. The witness has described a distinguishable tattoo that the attacker had on his chest, and WHITE has agreed to have a photograph of a tattoo on his chest taken for identification purposes. WHITE was photographed by a male police officer in the medical room and no other people were present. WHITE was made to remove only his shirt, and the tattoo on his chest was photographed. This was done without the presence of an appropriate adult, as WHITE had signified that he did not want one present.

Did the search and photographing of the tattoo comply with the Codes of Practice, in respect of dealing with juvenile detainees?

A Yes, as WHITE had signified that he did not want an appropriate adult present.

B No, there must *always* be at least one other person present, even if an appropriate adult does not have to be present.

C Yes, because the officer was not photographing intimate parts of the body, the presence of an appropriate adult was not necessary.

D No, because an appropriate adult should have been present in these circumstances.

Question 9.26

DING was arrested for being found drunk in a public place. He was so intoxicated that, when he arrived at the station, he was placed in a cell after being searched and fell asleep immediately. DING had nothing in his property which would have assisted in identifying him, therefore the arresting officer asked the custody officer whether DING could be examined without his consent, while he was asleep, to establish if he had any tattoos that might assist in identifying him.

Could an examination be authorised without DING's consent, under s. 54A of the Police and Criminal Evidence Act 1984, in these circumstances?

A Yes, because it was not practicable to obtain his consent.

B No, an examination may be conducted without a detainee's consent only where that person has refused to give consent.

C No, an examination may be conducted without consent only in cases of urgency.

D No, because the officer was not attempting to establish whether DING was a person who had been involved in the commission of an offence.

Question 9.27

KROL is a Russian national who has recently moved to the UK. His local police have been told that he has several convictions for child sex offences and that he is likely to continue committing offences in the UK. The police are concerned that as they do not have his fingerprints on record the public are at risk from him. The police wish to require KROL to attend at the police station to have his fingerprints taken. KROL has no convictions in the UK.

In relation to this which of the following is correct?

A Provided an inspector believes that this is necessary in the prevention of crime the requirement can be made.

B Provided a superintendent believes that this is necessary in the prevention of crime the requirement can be made.

C This requirement cannot be made as KROL is not from an EU Member State.

D This requirement cannot be made as KROL has no convictions in the UK.

ANSWERS

Answer 9.1

Answer **D** — The showing of a CCTV film used for security purposes is addressed at para. 3.28 of Code D.

Videos or photographs can be shown to the public at large through the national or local media, or to police officers for the purposes of recognition and tracing suspects. However, when such material is shown to potential witnesses (including police officers) it should be shown on an individual basis so as to avoid any possibility of collusion, and the showing shall, as far as possible, follow the principles for video identification if the suspect is known (paras 3.28, 3.29 and Annex A) or identification by photographs if the suspect is not known (see paras 3.3, 3.4 and Annex E).

It is important that where pictures or film are shown to specific police officers to try to identify suspects this must be done in a controlled way. In *R v Smith (Dean) and Others* [2008] EWCA Crim 1342, the court held that a police officer who was asked to view a CCTV recording to see if he could recognise any suspects involved in a robbery was not in the same shoes as a witness asked to identify someone he had seen committing a crime. However, safeguards that Code D was designed to put in place were equally important in cases where a police officer was asked to see whether he could recognise anyone in a CCTV recording. Whether or not Code D applied, there had to be in place some record that assisted in gauging the reliability of the assertion that the police officer recognised an individual. It was important that a police officer's initial reactions to viewing a CCTV recording were set out and available for scrutiny. Thus if the police officer failed to recognise anyone on first viewing but did so subsequently those circumstances ought to be noted. If a police officer failed to pick anybody else out that also should be recorded, as should any words of doubt. Furthermore, it was necessary that if recognition took place a record was made of what it was about the image that was said to have triggered the recognition. This is all the factors in our scenario; answers A, B and C are therefore incorrect as they limit what should be recorded.

Evidence and Procedure, paras 2.9.4.10, 2.9.12.1

Answer 9.2

Answer **D** — PACE Code D, para. 3.1 states:

A record shall be made of the suspect's description as first given by a potential witness. This record must:

(a) be made and kept in a form which enables details of that description to be accurately produced from it, in a visible and legible form, which can be given to the suspect or the suspect's solicitor in accordance with this Code...

So as it is legible then the handwritten note is the first description of the suspect and should be retained by the officer; there is nothing in the Code that states it needs to be signed and timed; answer C is therefore incorrect.

Although this description may be in the officer's PNB and the witness's statement neither of these will be the record of first description; answers A and B are therefore incorrect.

Evidence and Procedure, para. 2.9.4

Answer 9.3

Answer **C** — It is essential that once a person becomes a 'known suspect', he or she is afforded the rights and protection provided by PACE Code D. However, in this case the officer arrested the individual based on his own memory of the incident and not any 'street' identification. In this scenario the officer is a witness who then sees the suspect again, this is not an identification issue; answers A and B are therefore incorrect. Had the suspect been arrested by others and the witnessing officer been called to confirm his identity this would be a breach of Code D (*R v Lennon* (1999) 28 June, unreported).

However, the officer now cannot take part in any identification process as he arrested the suspect; answer D is therefore incorrect.

Evidence and Procedure, para. 2.9.4.4

Answer 9.4

Answer **D** — Code D requires that a first description provided of a person suspected of a crime (regardless of the time it was given) must be recorded (para. 3.1) and that a copy of the record should, where practicable (answers A and B are therefore incorrect), be given to the defence before certain procedures such as identification parades are carried out.

This record must be made and kept in a form which enables details of that description to be accurately produced from it, in a visible and legible form (Code D, para. 3.1), which can be given to the suspect or the suspect's solicitor; answer C is therefore incorrect.

Evidence and Procedure, para. 2.9.4

Answer 9.5

Answer **B** — Code D of the Police and Criminal Evidence Act 1984 Codes of Practice, paras 3.12 and 3.13 outlines circumstances in which an eyewitness identification procedure must be held:

> Whenever:
> (i) an eye witness has identified a suspect or purported to have identified them prior to any identification procedure set out in paragraphs 3.5 to 3.10 having been held; or
> (ii) there is a witness available, who expresses an ability to identify the suspect, or where there is a reasonable chance of the witness being able to do so, and they have not been given an opportunity to identify the suspect in any of the procedures set out in paragraphs 3.5 to 3.10, and the suspect disputes being the person the witness claims to have seen, an identification procedure shall be held unless it is not practicable or it would serve no useful purpose in proving or disproving whether the suspect was involved in committing the offence. For example, when it is not disputed that the suspect is already well known to the witness who claims to have seen them commit the crime.

Code D, para. 3.12(ii) provides that there is no need to go through any of the identification procedures where it is not practicable or it would serve no useful purpose in proving or disproving whether the suspect was involved in committing the offence. This view is supported by the Court of Appeal decision *R* v *Chen* [2001] EWCA Crim 885. The defence in that case was one of duress but the appeal was based on the failure of the police to hold identification procedures. The Court of Appeal stated that this was not a case about identification as none of the defendants denied their presence at the scene. What they denied was their criminal participation in the activities that took place. It followed, therefore, that Code D did not apply. Other examples would be where it is not in dispute that the suspect is already well known to the witness who claims to have seen the suspect commit the crime or where there is no reasonable possibility that a witness would be able to make an identification.

In this scenario if an identification procedure had been held, the officer would have picked NANCARROW out as the driver (as she knew not only him but another occupant of the car), making an identification procedure somewhat pointless, with no useful purpose; answers A and C are therefore incorrect.

However, attempts should be made to have the Dutch officer as a witness. Although several hundred miles away it is still practical (this might not be the case had he returned to Holland); answers A, C and D are therefore incorrect.

Evidence and Procedure, para. 2.9.4.5

Answer 9.6

Answer **D** — Code D, para. 3.12(ii) provides that there is no need to go through any of the identification procedures where it is not practicable or it would serve no useful purpose in proving or disproving whether the suspect was involved in committing the offence.

It is important to consider the distinction between identification of a suspect and the suspect's clothing or other features. In *D v DPP* (1998), The Times, 7 August, a witness had observed two youths for a continuous period of five to six minutes and then informed the police of what he had seen, describing the age of the youths and the clothes that they were wearing. The court held that there had not been an identification within the terms of the Codes of Practice because the witness had at no stage identified the defendant or the co-accused. He had described only their clothing and their approximate ages, and the police, acting on that information, had made the arrests. An identification parade could have served no useful purpose since the clothing would have been changed and those persons used for the parade would have been the same approximate age; answers A and B are therefore incorrect.

This point was further supported in *R v Haynes* [2004] EWCA Crim 390, where the Court of Appeal held that as a practical point the identification parade, whether or not the suspect was regarded as a known or unknown suspect, was of little value where the witness identified the suspect by clothing and not by recognition of the suspect's features. An identification parade would have provided little assistance.

Even accepting they were at the scene should a witness actually have described them then an identification parade may have had to have been held as it was their criminal participation that was disputed (*R v Chen* [2001] EWCA Crim 885); answer C is therefore incorrect.

Evidence and Procedure, para. 2.9.4.5

Answer 9.7

Answer **C** — Nothing in Code D of the PACE Codes of Practice inhibits showing films or photographs to the public through the national or local media, or to police officers for the purposes of recognition and tracing suspects.

When a broadcast or publication is made, a copy of the relevant material released to the media for the purposes of recognising or tracing the suspect, shall be kept.

The suspect or their solicitor shall be allowed to view such material before any identification procedure is carried out, provided it is practicable; answers A, B and D are therefore incorrect.

Evidence and Procedure, para. 2.9.4

Answer 9.8

Answer **D** — Generally, a witness may give evidence identifying the defendant's voice (*R* v *Robb* (1991) 93 Cr App R 161), while expert testimony may be admitted in relation to tape recordings of a voice which is alleged to belong to the defendant.

In *R* v *Flynn*; *R* v *St John* [2008] EWCA Crim 970 the Court of Appeal held that where the voice identification is from a recording, a prerequisite for making a speaker identification was that there should be a sample of an adequate size from the disputed recording that could confidently be attributed to a single speaker, not identifiable (answer A is therefore incorrect).

The court also recognised that expert evidence showed that lay listeners with considerable familiarity of a voice and listening to a clear recording could still make mistakes. It is therefore suggested other supporting evidence will be needed for a conviction to succeed; answers B and C are therefore incorrect.

Evidence and Procedure, para. 2.9.4.13

Answer 9.9

Answer **B** — Naturally, a person can consent to having his or her fingerprints taken at any time; the law deals with occasions where such consent is missing. Such cases are covered by s. 61 of the Police and Criminal Evidence Act 1984. Under s. 61(4), fingerprints of a person detained at a police station may be taken without that person's consent in the following two circumstances:

(4) The fingerprints of a person detained at a police station may be taken without the appropriate consent if—
   (a) he has been charged with a recordable offence or informed that he will be reported for such an offence; and
   (b) he has not had his fingerprints taken in the course of the investigation of the offence by the police.

As his fingerprints have already been taken, they cannot be taken again without consent or inspector's authority; answers A, C and D are therefore incorrect. Although in certain circumstances fingerprints can be taken without consent, this question is clearly aimed at where fingerprints will be taken with consent. Clearly fingerprints taken without consent will only apply where consent has been sought and not given.

Evidence and Procedure, para. 2.9.5

Answer 9.10

Answer **D** — The law around taking and retaining fingerprints has changed twice since the 1984 Act. The Criminal Justice and Police Act 2001 amended PACE to provide the police with the power to retain DNA and fingerprints relating to persons following acquittal at court or discontinuance of a case. The Criminal Justice Act 2003 further amended PACE to provide the police in England and Wales with additional powers to take and retain DNA and fingerprints from all persons detained at a police station having been arrested for a recordable offence. The Protection of Freedoms Act 2012, which came into force on 31 October 2013, has created a number of situations whereby police are no longer able to retain fingerprints and DNA.

Prior to the 2001 Act answer B would have been correct and prior to the 2012 Act answer A would have been correct. However, as the law now stands there are qualifying reasons to retain or destroy fingerprints; answers A and B are therefore incorrect.

The retention, where there is a charge but not a conviction, is determined by whether the person was charged with a qualifying offence or a minor offence.

- If the individual was charged with a qualifying offence, then the police can retain his data for three years (not five; answer C is therefore incorrect).
- If the individual was charged with a minor offence he will have his fingerprints deleted automatically.

Evidence and Procedure, para. 2.9.13.1

Answer 9.11

Answer **D** — In *R (On the application of Howe) and Law Society (Interested Party)* v *South Durham Magistrates' Court and CPS (Interested Party)* [2004] EWHC 362 (Admin) the claimant was charged with driving while disqualified and without insurance. At no time did he admit that he was the Christopher Howe who had been disqualified. As it was necessary for the prosecution to prove that the defendant before the court was the person disqualified from driving, the prosecution applied for a witness summons to be issued to a solicitor, who had been the solicitor acting for the Christopher Howe who was disqualified and who was also acting for the claimant in respect of the present charge. This was opposed citing that the issuing of the summons would involve a breach of legal professional privilege, also that it would violate the claimant's rights under Art. 6 of the European Convention on Human Rights by depriving him of his right to be represented by a lawyer of his choice and that it would conflict with his right not to incriminate himself.

The Administrative Court held that questions solely as to the identity of the person disqualified from driving in the original court hearing and as to the identification of the claimant as being that person did not infringe legal professional privilege; answer A is therefore incorrect. The admissible question would be whether, when the solicitor first saw the claimant in connection with the prosecution, he knew him or remembered him. The solicitor was not being called in his capacity as the claimant's solicitor, but as a person who was present in court at the relevant time. With regard to the argument that the claimant would be deprived of the solicitor of his choice, although that was important it was not an absolute right and there was no risk of injustice to the claimant if he was required to make a fresh choice of solicitor; answer B is therefore incorrect.

The court was 'mystified' by the dilemma supposedly faced by the claimant's solicitor. After all, if this witness could categorically state that their client was not the person disqualified this would have a devastating effect on the prosecution case. However, if they knew the person to be disqualified, it would be embarrassing to admit they represented them knowing they were indeed guilty.

As a cautionary warning, however, the court did not view this case as any sort of licence to increase the amount of such applications by the CPS, and stated that calling a solicitor in such circumstances must only be a last resort; answer C is therefore incorrect.

Evidence and Procedure, para. 2.9.4.14

Answer 9.12

Answer **D** — DNA extracted from blood or semen stains, or even from body hairs, etc., found at the scene of the crime or on the victim is compared with samples (typically derived from mouth swabs) taken from the suspect. The process has been refined in recent years, but is essentially similar to that described by Lord Taylor CJ in *R v Deen*, The Times, 10 January 1994. A positive match between the two profiles does not necessarily provide comparable proof of guilt, and the courts have made it clear that DNA evidence alone will not be sufficient for a conviction; there needs to be other supporting evidence to link the suspect to the crime, and answer A is therefore incorrect. This may be any supporting evidence linking the suspect to the area or circumstances of the crime, or may come from questions put to the suspect during interview. It would include circumstantial evidence, i.e. being seen in the area. It need not be direct evidence gained by other identification procedures or otherwise; answers B and C are therefore incorrect. In *R* v *Lashley* [2000] EWCA Crim 88, in addition to the DNA evidence, evidence that the suspect had connections in the area was enough for the jury to consider the likelihood that the defendant was the assailant.

Evidence and Procedure, para. 2.9.7.1

Answer 9.13

Answer **A** — The definition of an intimate sample is:

- a sample of blood, semen, or any other tissue fluid, urine or pubic hair;
- a dental impression;
- a swab taken from any part of a person's genitals or from a person's body orifice other than the mouth.

The definition of a non-intimate sample is:

- a sample of hair, other than pubic hair, which includes hair plucked with the root;
- a sample taken from a nail or from under a nail;
- a swab taken from any part of a person's body including the mouth but not any other body orifice other than a part from which a swab taken would be an intimate sample;
- saliva;
- a skin impression which means any record, other than a fingerprint, which is a record, in any form and produced by any method, of a skin pattern and other physical characteristics or features of the whole, or any part of, a person's foot or of any other part of his/her body.

So a swab from a person's penis would be an intimate sample and the Serious Organised Crime and Police Act 2005 has extended the definition beyond a 'body orifice', although it has not gone as far as declaring the penis to be a body orifice; answer B is therefore incorrect. Answer D is almost correct, apart from the caveat in the definition that states 'a swab taken from any part of a person's body including the mouth but not any other body orifice other than a part from which a swab taken would be an intimate sample'; answers C and D are therefore incorrect as a penile swab is an intimate sample.

Evidence and Procedure, para. 2.9.7

Answer 9.14

Answer **C** — Paragraph 6.9 of Code D of the Police and Criminal Evidence Act 1984 Codes of Practice sets out the provisions to be followed where clothing needs to be removed in circumstances likely to cause embarrassment. These are:

- no person of the opposite sex may be present (other than a registered medical practitioner or registered health care professional);
- only people whose presence is necessary for the taking of the sample should in fact be present;
- in the case of a juvenile or mentally disordered or mentally vulnerable person, an appropriate adult of the opposite sex may be present *if specifically requested by the person and the person is readily available;*
- in the case of a juvenile, clothing may only be removed in the absence of an appropriate adult if the person signifies (in the presence of the appropriate adult) that he/she prefers his/her absence and the appropriate adult agrees.
- Clearly, as consent is needed to take a sample, the use of force would be inappropriate.

In the case of a juvenile the appropriate adult need not be present if the juvenile signifies (in the presence of the appropriate adult) that he/she prefers his/her absence and the appropriate adult agrees; as the agreement of the adult is required, answer A is incorrect.

In this scenario although the juvenile did not want an appropriate adult present, and the adult agreed, this conversation would have had to take place with the adult present, which he/she was not; answer B is therefore incorrect. An adult does not have to be present when an intimate sample is taken, provided both the juvenile and the adult agree; answer D is therefore incorrect.

Evidence and Procedure, para. 2.9.7

Answer 9.15

Answer **B** — By s. 63(3ZA) of the Police and Criminal Evidence Act 1984, a non-intimate sample may be taken without the appropriate consent from a person who has been arrested for a recordable offence and released if the person:

(i) is on bail and has not had a sample of the same type and from the same part of the body taken in the course of the investigation of the offence, or;

(ii) has had such a sample taken in the course of the investigation of the offence, but it proved unsuitable or insufficient.

PACE, s. 63A(4) and sch. 2A provide powers to make a requirement (in accordance with Code D Annex G) for a person to attend a police station to have a non-intimate sample taken in accordance with s. 63(3ZA) provided the requirement was not made more than six months from the day the investigating officer was informed that the sample previously taken was unsuitable or insufficient; answers A, C and D are therefore incorrect.

Evidence and Procedure, para. 2.9.7

Answer 9.16

Answer **B** — Section 62 of PACE sets out police powers in relation to intimate samples, and the circumstances under which they may be obtained. They are subject to the consent of the person, as well as authorisation by the appropriate police officer. The Criminal Justice and Police Act 2001, s. 80(1) lowered the level of authority from superintendent to inspector; therefore answer C is incorrect. This authority remains at the same level irrespective of whether the person is in police detention or not, as outlined in Code D, para. 6.2; therefore, answers A and D are incorrect.

Evidence and Procedure, para. 2.9.7

Answer 9.17

Answer **D** — An officer of at least the rank of inspector (or the court) may authorise taking the fingerprints of a person who has answered bail at a court or police station, if the person answering bail has done so on behalf of a person whose fingerprints were taken on a previous occasion and there are reasonable grounds for believing that he or she is not the same person, or the person claims to be a different person from a person whose fingerprints were taken previously (s. 61(4A) and (4B) of the Police and Criminal Evidence Act 1984).

Since this power relates to a person answering bail at a police station as well as a court, answer A is incorrect. Answers A and B are also incorrect because the power may be utilised before a person has been charged with an offence. The authority to take fingerprints in these circumstances may be given orally or in writing; but if given orally, it must be confirmed in writing as soon as is practicable. Answer C is therefore incorrect.

Evidence and Procedure, para. 2.9.5

Answer 9.18

Answer **C** — If a suspect is 'known' or is 'recognised' there may still be occasions where an identification procedure may need to be followed; answers A and B are therefore incorrect. In a world of social media it is not surprising that identifications are being made through this and are coming before the courts. In *R* v *Alexander and McGill* [2012] EWCA Crim 2768 the victim identified the suspects through their Facebook account pictures. The court observed that identifications done in this way, through the use of Facebook, were likely to rise and it was therefore incumbent upon investigators to take steps to obtain, in as much detail as possible, evidence in relation to the initial identification. In this case, before trial requests were made by the defence for photographs of the other Facebook pages that had been considered by the victim and his sister so that defendants could consider how their identifications might have been made. This means that showing of photographs in line with Annex E would not be correct and that the police should obtain as much detail as possible as to how the identification was made on social media; answer D is therefore incorrect.

Evidence and Procedure, paras 2.9.4.10, 2.9.12.1

Answer 9.19

Answer **A** — The PACE Codes of Practice, Code D, para. 6.1 provides the following definition of intimate and non-intimate samples:

(a) an 'intimate sample' means:
- a sample of blood, semen, or any other tissue fluid, urine or pubic hair;
- a dental impression;
- a swab taken from any part of a person's genitals or from a person's body orifice other than the mouth.

(b) a 'non-intimate sample' means:
- a sample of hair, other than pubic hair, which includes hair plucked with the root;
- a sample taken from a nail or from under a nail;
- a swab taken from any part of a person's body other than a part from which a swab taken would be an intimate sample;
- saliva;
- a skin impression which means any record, other than a fingerprint, which is a record, in any form and produced by any method, of the skin pattern and other physical characteristics or features of the whole, or any part of, a person's foot or of any other part of their body.

Answers B, C and D are *all* intimate samples; the question asked you to identify samples which were *not* classed as intimate samples, therefore if you selected any of these, the answer was incorrect. A skin impression which is not a fingerprint is a non-intimate sample.

Evidence and Procedure, para. 2.9.7

Answer 9.20

Answer **C** — Impressions of a person's footwear may be taken in connection with the investigation of an offence only with their consent or if Code D, para. 4.17 applies, which states:

> PACE, section 61A, provides power for a police officer to take footwear impressions without consent from any person over the age of ten years who is detained at a police station:
> (a) in consequence of being arrested for a recordable offence; or if the detainee has been charged with a recordable offence, or informed they will be reported for such an offence...

No consent is required and the impressions can be taken; answers A, B and D are therefore incorrect.

Evidence and Procedure, para. 2.9.5

Answer 9.21

Answer **B** — Code D, para. 6.9 of the PACE Codes of Practice outlines the provisions for taking an intimate sample, where clothing needs to be removed in circumstances likely to cause embarrassment. Paragraph 6.9 states:

> When clothing needs to be removed in circumstances likely to cause embarrassment to the person, no person of the opposite sex who is not a registered medical practitioner or registered health care professional shall be present (unless in the case of a juvenile, mentally disordered or mentally vulnerable person, that person specifically requests the presence of an appropriate adult of the opposite sex who is readily available) nor shall anyone whose presence is unnecessary.

However, in the case of a juvenile, this is subject to the overriding proviso that such a removal of clothing may take place in the absence of the appropriate adult only if the juvenile signifies, in their presence, that they prefer the adult's absence and they agree.

Answer A is incorrect; the decision was made by MURPHY when his mother was not present and she should have been consulted in respect of that decision. The fact that MURPHY's mother was not readily available is immaterial—this issue is only relevant when a juvenile, mentally disordered or mentally vulnerable person specifically requests the *presence* of an appropriate adult of the opposite sex who is readily available, therefore answer C is incorrect. Paragraph 6.9 applies to *all* juveniles under 17, therefore answer D is incorrect.

Evidence and Procedure, para. 2.9.7

Answer 9.22

Answer **D** — Code D requires that a first description provided of a person suspected of a crime (regardless of the time it was given) must be recorded (para. 3.1) and that a copy of the record should, where practicable, be given to the defence before certain procedures such as identification parades are carried out.

This record must be made and kept in a form which enables details of that description to be accurately produced from it, in a visible and legible form (Code D, para. 3.1), which can be given to the suspect or the suspect's solicitor. Such a record could be made electronically or be paper-based; answers A, B and C are therefore incorrect.

Evidence and Procedure, para. 2.9.4

Answer 9.23

Answer **A** — Section 64A of the Police and Criminal Evidence Act 1984 has been amended by the Serious and Organised Crime and Police Act 2005. This means that a person who is detained at a police station or elsewhere than at a police station may be photographed with his or her consent; or if it is withheld or it is not practicable to obtain it, without his or her consent (guidance is provided in Code D, paras 5.12 to 5.18). This applies to all persons who are in police detention, and not just those charged or reported for an offence; therefore answer D is incorrect.

Code D, para. 5.12 sets out the circumstances where a person who is not detained at a police station may be photographed.

Photographs can be taken with or without consent (although consent should be asked for). Code D, paras 5.12 to 5.18 outline these requirements. As photographs can be taken without consent, answer B is incorrect. A photograph taken under s. 64A may be used by, or disclosed to, any person for any purpose related to the prevention or detection of crime, the investigation of an offence or the conduct of a prosecution or the enforcement of a sentence. Code D, Note 5B gives examples where such photographs may be of use. The use of the photograph is for any conduct which constitutes a criminal offence (whether under UK law or in another country). This therefore allows the photograph to be used in the preparation of any identification procedure that is being arranged involving the suspect (Code D, para. 3.30); answer C is therefore incorrect.

Evidence and Procedure, para. 2.9.6

Answer 9.24

Answer **C** — The authority to search detainees and examine them to ascertain their identity is contained in s. 54A of the Police and Criminal Evidence Act 1984. An officer of at least the rank of inspector may authorise a person to be searched or examined in order to ascertain if the person has any mark that would tend to identify him or her as a person involved in the commission of an offence, or any mark that would assist to identify him or her (including showing that he or she is not a particular person). Answers A and B are therefore incorrect. Authority may be given either orally or in writing, provided it is confirmed in writing as soon as practicable (see Code D, para. 5.2). Answer D is therefore incorrect.

Evidence and Procedure, para. 2.9.6

Answer 9.25

Answer **D** — The authority to search detainees and examine them to ascertain their identity is contained in s. 54A of the Police and Criminal Evidence Act 1984 and governed by Code D, paras 5.1 to 5.11. Note that this power can be authorised by an inspector where consent is absent, although where consent is given it must be proper consent. For a juvenile aged 14 or over this must be his or her consent, and that of the appropriate adult. The search, if it involves the removal of more than the person's outer clothing, will be conducted in accordance with Code C, Annex A, para. 11 (strip searches). Paragraph 11(c) states that except in cases of urgency, where there is a risk of serious harm to the detainee or others (which is not the case in the scenario), a search of a juvenile may take place in the absence of an appropriate adult only if the juvenile signifies in the presence of the appropriate adult that he or she does not want the adult to be present during the search, and the appropriate adult agrees; therefore answer A is incorrect. Thus, even though the officer was not photographing intimate parts of the body, because this case involved a juvenile, the consent of both the detainee and the appropriate adult must be obtained; answer C is therefore incorrect. If an appropriate adult is not present without appropriate consent, there need to be at least two people present during the search only where intimate parts of the body may be exposed; answer B is therefore incorrect.

Evidence and Procedure, para. 2.9.6

Answer 9.26

Answer **D** — The authority to search detainees and examine them to ascertain their identity is contained in s. 54A of the Police and Criminal Evidence Act 1984 and Code D, para. 5. An officer of at least the rank of inspector may authorise a person to be searched or examined for two general purposes, namely, in order to ascertain if the person:

- has any mark that would tend to identify him or her as a person involved in the commission of an offence (para. 5(1)(a)); *or*
- has any mark that would assist to identify him or her (including showing that he or she is not a particular person) (para. 5(1)(b)).

The detainee in the scenario would fall within para. 5(1)(b). Searches and examinations may be conducted without the person's consent in order to identify him or her for either of the previous reasons. However, the requirements are different, depending on the paragraph concerned. A search or examination under para. 5(1)(a) may be carried out without the person's consent only when consent is withheld, or it is not practicable to obtain consent. A search or examination under para. 5(1)(b) (which is applicable to the scenario) may be carried out without the person's consent only when the detainee has refused to identify himself or herself, or the authorising officer has reasonable grounds for suspecting that the person is not who he or she claims to be.

Returning to the scenario, the detainee had not been given the opportunity to refuse to identify himself, therefore a search under this section could not take place at this time. As can be seen previously, the search could not be authorised because it was not practicable to obtain his consent, because this requirement only applies to detainees who fall within para. 5(1)(a). Answer A is therefore incorrect.

Answer B is incorrect because, as can be seen previously, an examination may be conducted without a detainee's consent for reasons other than where a person has simply refused to give consent.

Lastly, an examination without a detainee's consent may be authorised for any of the reasons listed previously. There is no mention in the Codes of Practice of 'urgent' cases. Answer C is therefore incorrect.

(Note that reasonable force may be used, if necessary, to carry out a search or examination under this section.)

Evidence and Procedure, para. 2.9.6

Answer 9.27

Answer **A** — The Police and Criminal Evidence Act 1984, s. 61, provides powers to take fingerprints without consent from any person over the age of 10 years. Section 61(6D) allows this from a person who has been convicted outside England and Wales of an offence which if committed in England and Wales would be a qualifying offence as defined by PACE, s. 65A (serious offences) if:

(i) the person's fingerprints have not been taken previously under this power or their fingerprints have been so taken on a previous occasion but they do not constitute a complete set or some, or all, of the fingerprints are not of sufficient quality to allow satisfactory analysis, comparison or matching; and

(ii) a police officer of inspector rank or above is satisfied that taking fingerprints is necessary to assist in the prevention or detection of crime and authorises them to be taken.

This power is not limited to citizens of EU Member States; answer C is therefore incorrect. It is immaterial that this person has no UK convictions; answer D is therefore incorrect.

The authorisation is at inspector level not superintendent; answer B is therefore incorrect.

PACE, s. 63A(4) gives power to require the person to attend at the police station to have fingerprints taken.

Evidence and Procedure, para. 2.9.5

10 | Interviews

STUDY PREPARATION

Another area of direct practical relevance to all police officers is that of interviews of suspects. This area is heavily regulated by the Police and Criminal Evidence Act 1984 and the Codes of Practice.

Key aspects of this area are:

- cautioning;
- interview procedure at police stations and elsewhere;
- access to legal advisers; and
- interviews with vulnerable people, the use of interpreters and emergency.

QUESTIONS

Question 10.1

Constable DREW is on patrol in a vehicle carrying ANPR. A vehicle passes and the ANPR alerts Constable DREW to the fact that the vehicle is reported lost or stolen. The officer pulls alongside the vehicle and notices an elderly couple are the only occupants. The officer tries to do a PNC check but the system is unavailable. The officer suspects that the vehicle is not stolen due to the age of the occupants. Constable DREW stops the vehicle and says to the driver 'Who is the vehicle registered to?'

In these circumstances should the officer have cautioned the driver as outlined in Code C of the Police and Criminal Evidence Act 1984?

A Yes, as the vehicle is stolen and there are grounds to suspect an offence has been committed.

B Yes, as the vehicle is stolen the officer must caution the driver even if only asking questions about ownership.

C No, as the officer does not suspect the driver of committing an offence he need not caution him.

D No, questions only to establish ownership of a vehicle never need be prefaced with a caution.

Question 10.2

Constable HAWKINS is dealing with an offence of theft, where a man is suspected to have been stealing from his mother. The man attends voluntarily at the police station and explains to the police support staff inquiry officer that he is 'there to be interviewed about a theft, but they'll never find where I've hidden the jewellery'. The man laughed out loud and winked at the inquiry officer. The inquiry officer believed the man to be joking with her.

Was what the man said to the inquiry officer a 'significant statement' as outlined in Code C, para. 11.4 of the Police and Criminal Evidence Act 1984 Codes of Practice?

A Yes, it appears capable of being used in evidence against him.

B Yes, it was said within the confines of a police station, and to a police officer or police staff.

C No, it was not said to a police officer; police staff are not mentioned in the relevant code.

D No, it is not a confession, and does not relate to a direct admission of guilt.

Question 10.3

Police officers have been called by the principal of a high school to interview a juvenile who has caused damage to school property. The principal did not witness the incident, but wishes the juvenile to be interviewed on the school premises as the youth is due to sit a GCSE in two hours. The parents of the juvenile have been contacted, but are unavailable for some time.

Can the principal be the 'appropriate adult'?

A In these circumstances, only the principal can be the appropriate adult.

B The principal can be the appropriate adult as the parents are not readily available.

C The principal can be the appropriate adult provided the parents agree.

D The principal will not be able to be the appropriate adult in these circumstances.

Question 10.4

PUDDY is being interviewed for an offence of burglary. During a break he tells the interviewing officer that he wants to object to the interview being audibly recorded.

What action should the officer now take?

A The officer must record the suspect's objections on the tape and then switch it off.

B The officer must state on the tape that the interview will no longer be recorded and that a written record will now be made and then switch the tape off.

C The officer should record the suspect's objections on the tape; however, it is their decision whether to proceed with the audio recording still on.

D The officer should state on the tape that an objection has been raised; however, it is their decision whether to proceed with the audio recording still on.

Question 10.5

Constable HIGGINS has been interviewing a suspect at length about an offence and is about to start another interview after a break for lunch. The officer reminds the suspect they are under caution but does not give the caution again.

In relation to this which of the following is correct in accordance with the Codes of Practice?

A The officer should stop the recording until they have cautioned the suspect again.

B The officer should caution the suspect again should there be any doubt he/she are not aware they are still under caution.

C The officer has fully complied with the Code in reminding the suspect he/she are under caution, as there are no other requirements under the Code.

D The officer has fully complied with the Code in reminding the suspect he/she are under caution as the suspect's solicitor is present at the interview.

Question 10.6

Detectives are questioning a suspect arrested on suspicion of kidnap and murder. There have been several interviews and during the last one the suspect refused to answer a question about being seen on CCTV near the scene of the kidnap. The officers are about to interview the suspect again.

In relation to the refusal to answer the question in the last interview, which of the following is correct?

A The interviewers should ask the suspect to confirm that in the previous interview he refused to answer the question about the CCTV.

B The interviewers should ask the suspect to confirm that in the previous interview he refused to answer the question about the CCTV and ask if he wishes to add anything.

C The officers should not mention the previous refusal to answer questions as it was not a significant statement.

D The officers should not mention the previous refusal to answer as it is not capable of being used in evidence against the suspect.

Question 10.7

STODDARD has been arrested and is in custody at the police station suspected of a series of rapes; this followed a description obtained from his various victims; a first description was obtained and recorded. The suspect has, in accordance with his rights, asked for his solicitor to be called. Prior to the arrival of his solicitor STOD-DARD is examined by the police surgeon and samples obtained. Officers also attend at STODDARD's home address and carry out a search in compliance with s. 18 of the Police and Criminal Evidence Act 1984 and various items are seized as being of evidential value. Prior to the first interview the interview co-ordinator is considering what will be disclosed to STODDARD's solicitor.

In relation to the various items obtained what *must* be disclosed to the solicitor at this stage of the investigation?

A Only the custody record.

B The custody record, and the record of first description.

C The custody record, the record of first description and the details of the items seized.

D At this stage, there is no mandatory disclosure, it is discretionary for the investigating officer.

Question 10.8

Detective Sergeant STROUD is carrying out a visually recorded interview with a suspect for murder. The suspect is a well-known gang member and fearing for his own safety, Detective Sergeant STROUD wishes to hide his identity and sit with his back to the camera. There have been no specific threats made against Detective Sergeant STROUD, however, the gang members have issued a generic warning to any officer concerned in the investigation of the murder.

In relation to the correct procedure, which of the following is true?

A The officer can do this, but must record on the interview record the reasons for this.

B The officer can do this, but must record on the custody record or in his pocket notebook the reasons for doing this.

C The officer cannot do this as the suspect is not a person detained under the Terrorism Act 2000.

D The officer cannot do this as no specific threat has been made against him.

Question 10.9

MORE is being interviewed by detectives in relation to an allegation of fraud. During the audio-recorded interview, MORE alleges that his rights under PACE Code C were breached and that he wishes to make a formal complaint.

Which of the following is correct?

A The audio recording should be stopped and an inspector summoned to deal with the complaint.

B The custody officer is responsible for deciding whether the interview should continue or not in these circumstances.

C The interviewing officer should make a note in his or her pocket notebook, and later, on the custody record, of the complaint.

D The custody officer should be summoned immediately, and the audio recording left running until he or she arrives.

Question 10.10

Constable VENISON was interviewing GOUDY, who had been arrested the previous evening for an assault. During the interview the recording equipment fails and attempts to use new tapes are not successful. There are no other recording facilities readily available.

What action should Constable VENISON now take?

A The interview will have to wait until recording facilities become available and the officer should note on the new media the reasons for the delay.

B The interview will have to wait until recording facilities become available and the officer should précis the original interview prior to proceeding with the new one.

C The interview may continue without being audibly recorded. If this happens, the interviewer shall seek the custody officer's authority.

D The interview may continue without being audibly recorded. If this happens, the interviewer shall seek authority of an officer not below the rank of inspector.

Question 10.11

Detective Constables GRAINGER and SADDIQUE were interviewing PARKES for an offence of murder. The interview was being visually recorded. About an hour into the interview, the officers decided to have a short break and Detective Constable GRAINGER left the interview room to obtain refreshments, leaving Detective Constable SADDIQUE alone in the room with PARKES.

What advice is contained in the PACE Codes of Practice, Code F, paras 4.12 and 4.13, as to whether or not the video recording equipment should be turned off in these circumstances?

A It *must* not be turned off, because PARKES and another police officer have remained in the interview room.

B It *may* be turned off, because one of the interviewing officers has left the interview room.

C It *must* be turned off, because one of the interviewing officers has left the interview room.

D It *must* be turned off and the recording media removed, because one of the interviewing officers has left the interview room.

Question 10.12

Constable DAVIES is interviewing EDDISON (who is accompanied by his solicitor) on tape at a non-designated police station for a common assault offence. Her colleague, Constable POBOWSKI is acting as custody officer, the nearest inspector is six miles away. At the conclusion of the interview the solicitor refuses to sign the master recording label although EDDISON does sign the label.

What action should Constable DAVIES now take?

A She should note the fact the solicitor has refused to sign; no further action is required as the suspect did sign the label.

B She should call in Constable POBOWSKI who should sign the label.

C She should call in Constable POBOWSKI who should sign the label, only after seeking authority from the inspector to do so.

D She should write 'third party refused to sign' on the label, and sign that entry.

Question 10.13

DRURY has been arrested for a series of burglaries and has been in custody for some time and is being put into a rest period. After 2 hours his solicitor arrives and requests an urgent consultation with his client.

In relation to this which of the following is correct?

A As this is an urgent request it should be allowed and after consultation a fresh 8-hour rest period should be given.

B Any request from a legal adviser should be granted and after consultation a fresh 8-hour rest period should be given.

C As this is an urgent request it should be allowed and after consultation a fresh 6-hour rest period should be given.

D Any request from a legal adviser should be granted and after consultation a fresh 6-hour rest period should be given.

Question 10.14

Officers are about to interview YOUNG in relation to a robbery offence. The officers are also planning to hold an identification procedure later after they have carried out this interview. They have a first description of the suspect that was obtained from a witness to the offence, and YOUNG is represented by a legal adviser.

Must the officers disclose this first description to the suspect and his solicitor?

A Yes, as they know an identification procedure will follow.

B Yes, but only if they intend asking him questions about this description.

C No, there is no requirement to provide the first description at this stage.

D No, a first description need only be supplied after an identification procedure is held.

Question 10.15

GODDARD has been arrested for murder and is represented at police interview by his legal adviser. The solicitor asks the police to provide the cause of death as part of their disclosure to him but the police refuse. He therefore advises his client to exercise his right to silence as he cannot properly advise his client as he does not know the cause of death.

Which of the following is correct in relation to adverse inferences that could be drawn due to this silence at interview?

A Inferences could be drawn as GODDARD must put forward a defence even where his solicitor advises silence.

B Inferences should not be drawn as the officers must disclose the cause of death.

C Inferences should not be drawn as the officers should give basic information, and the cause of death would be basic information.

D Inferences should not be drawn as GODDARD refused to answer questions on his solicitor's advice.

Question 10.16

Officers are carrying out a series of interviews in relation to a complex fraud investigation and need to build in breaks to their interview schedule.

How long should a meal break normally last?

A At least 30 minutes.

B At least 45 minutes.

C At least one hour.

D At least one hour 15 minutes.

Question 10.17

Officers are interviewing a suspect using video recording of the interviews and are using certified recording media.

What should the certified recording material have superimposed on it?

A The duration time of the interview.

B The date and duration time of the interview.

C The date and time of the interview.

D The date, time and duration time of the interview.

Question 10.18

Constable CONWAY is interviewing a suspect suspected of theft. The officer has gained a significant amount of evidence and is wondering at what point in time the interview should be concluded.

When should the officer conclude the interview?

A When there is sufficient evidence to provide a realistic prospect of conviction.

B When there is sufficient evidence to prosecute.

C When there is sufficient evidence to charge.

D When the officer considers that they have asked all relevant questions.

Question 10.19

GREENING is suffering from a significant mental disorder but is suspected of being involved in a case where a young girl was kidnapped. The girl has not been found but GREENING has been arrested and an appropriate adult will not be available for at least two hours. Police officers wish to urgently interview GREENING to prevent harm to the girl and the superintendent is considering the matter.

Which of the following is correct?

A GREENING can be interviewed provided his solicitor is present during the interview.

B GREENING can be interviewed provided the superintendent believes the interview would not significantly harm GREENING's mental state.

C GREENING cannot be interviewed under any circumstances without an appropriate adult being present.

D GREENING cannot be interviewed unless a mental health professional agrees it would not significantly harm his mental health.

Question 10.20

Constable DE MARCO is investigating an assault involving a wounding. The complainant states that WATERS had stabbed him in the arm with a knife in the street outside his house; WATERS then used the knife to cut his hand and rubbed this across the wound he had caused in the complainant's arm. WATERS said 'now you have HIV as well as me'. The officer went to WATERS' address and arrested him, seizing a blood stained knife. During the interview WATERS stated he had cut his hand whilst chopping an onion but said 'no comment' to questions about the knife.

In these circumstances can a special warning under s. 36 of the Criminal Justice and Public Order Act 1994 be given?

A Yes, in relation to the cut on WATERS' hand and also the knife.

B Yes, in relation to the knife only.

C No, the knife was not 'found' at a place at or about the time the offence for which he was arrested is alleged to have been committed.

D No, the cut is not a 'mark' as defined in s. 36 and therefore not subject to a special warning.

Question 10.21

DICKENS makes a complaint to the police about a robbery. During the struggle DICKENS states he bit the perpetrator on the hand, enough to probably leave teeth marks. The police suspect FRENCH and arrest him in the street, and he has bite marks on his hand. A lawfully conducted search of his house finds items stolen from DICKENS. During interview he refuses to answer questions about the property found in his house, and states he was bitten by his girlfriend during sex.

In relation to s. 36 of the Criminal Justice and Public Order Act 1994 can the police give FRENCH a 'special warning'?

A Yes, in relation to the teeth marks only.

B Yes, in relation to the property found only.

C Yes, in relation to both the teeth marks and the property found.

D No, the police cannot give a special warning for either the teeth marks or the property found.

Question 10.22

CHIBA is on trial for an offence of rape, and has been sworn to give evidence. Prosecuting counsel asks him, 'It is true, is it not, that you did have sexual intercourse with Miss DAVIES, and at that time you clearly knew that she did not consent?' CHIBA remains silent, and refuses to answer the question.

Will the jury be entitled to draw any inferences from CHIBA's refusal to answer this question?

A No, CHIBA has a right not to incriminate himself and inferences may not be drawn.

B No, the prosecution have no right to ask such questions, and inferences may not be drawn.

C Yes, CHIBA has refused without good cause to answer the question, and inferences may be drawn.

D Yes, and the inferences drawn from this refusal would be enough to convict.

Question 10.23

AKITA was the driver of a vehicle involved in a fatal road traffic collision. He was taken to hospital where he refused to give a sample of blood under the 'hospital procedure' as set out by s. 9 of the Road Traffic Act 1988 as he has a fear of needles. He was arrested for causing death by dangerous driving and interviewed when deemed fit. Acting on solicitor's advice he remained silent in response to the limited questions asked. Following extensive investigation during which several witnesses claimed AKITA had drunk copious amounts of alcohol and was driving in excess of 90 mph at the time of the collision, he was again interviewed three months after the collision. Again acting on solicitor's advice, he remained silent. At his trial AKITA gave evidence that he had drunk very little alcohol and was driving within the speed limit. His counsel argued that no inferences could be drawn on his silence at the first interview due to lack of evidence disclosed by the police to him and no inferences could be drawn on his silence on the second interview as it should not have been held as the police had at that time sufficient evidence to charge.

In relation to whether inferences could be drawn from his silence during his two interviews which of the following is correct?

A No inferences from first interview only as the solicitor advised silence due to lack of disclosure of evidence by the police.

B No inferences from second interview only because the second interview should not have been held; he should have been charged.

C No inferences drawn from either due to lack of disclosure of evidence and that no second interview should have been held; he should have been charged.

D Inferences could be drawn from both interviews as they were both properly conducted.

ANSWERS

Answer 10.1

Answer **C** — The Police and Criminal Evidence Act 1984, Code C, para. 10.1 states:

> A person whom there are grounds to suspect of an offence, must be cautioned before any questions about an offence, or further questions if the answers provide the grounds for suspicion, are put to them if either the suspect's answers or silence, (i.e. failure or refusal to answer or answer satisfactorily) may be given in evidence to a court in a prosecution. A person need not be cautioned if questions are for other necessary purposes, e.g.:
> (a) solely to establish their identity or ownership of any vehicle...

So although there are grounds to suspect the vehicle is stolen (the ANPR report), what is vital is the officer's belief about the person they are about to question. Here the officer does not suspect the driver of stealing the car and therefore need not caution him; answers A and B are therefore incorrect.

Note that the Code states that a person need not be cautioned to establish ownership of a vehicle; however, that is not always clear-cut where the vehicle is stolen. In this scenario, had the officer suspected the driver of stealing the car then there would be grounds to suspect him of an offence and a caution must be given. Where such suspicion exists questions about ownership form part of an interview about the offence, and are subject to caution; answer D is therefore incorrect. Had the officer suspected that the driver was in possession of drugs then a caution to establish identity/ownership need not be given as those questions do not relate to the offence under suspicion.

Evidence and Procedure, para. 2.10.2

Answer 10.2

Answer **A** — At the beginning of an interview the interviewer, after cautioning the suspect, shall put to him/her any significant statement or silence which occurred in the presence and hearing of a police officer or other police staff before the start of the interview and which have not been put to the suspect in the course of a previous interview. The interviewer shall ask the suspect whether he/she confirms or denies that earlier statement or silence and if he/she wants to add anything.

A significant statement is one which appears capable of being used in evidence against the suspect, in particular a direct admission of guilt.

Whether a joke or not the statement made by the suspect would be capable of being given in evidence against him/her even though it was not a direct admission of guilt (although arguably it is!); answer D is therefore incorrect.

The statement can be made anywhere (not just a police station) and can be said to police staff as well as police officers; answers B and C are therefore incorrect.

Evidence and Procedure, para. 2.10.3

Answer 10.3

Answer **D** — Interviews at educational establishments should take place only in exceptional circumstances and with the agreement of the principal or the principal's nominee (PACE Code C, para. 11.16). This is the mandatory practice; however, it is not mandatory that the principal be the appropriate adult, and therefore answer A is incorrect. If waiting for the parents (or other appropriate adult) to attend would cause unreasonable delay, the principal can be the appropriate adult, and this is not dependent on the parents' consent and therefore answer C is incorrect. The only exception to this is where the juvenile is suspected of an offence against his or her educational establishment, as the youth is in the question. In these circumstances the principal cannot be the appropriate adult and answer B is therefore incorrect (Code C, para. 11.16).

Evidence and Procedure, para. 2.10.3.2

Answer 10.4

Answer **C** — If a suspect objects to the interview being audibly recorded at the outset, during the interview or during a break, the interviewer shall explain that the interview is being audibly recorded and that the code requires the suspect's objections to be recorded on the audio recording.

When any objections have been audibly recorded or the suspect has refused to have their objections recorded, the interviewer shall say they are turning off the recorder, give their reasons and turn it off. It is the suspect who must be given an opportunity to raise their objections or refuse, not the officer; answers B and D are therefore incorrect.

If, however, the interviewer reasonably considers it necessary they may proceed to question the suspect with the audio recording still on; answer A is therefore incorrect.

Evidence and Procedure, para. 2.10.10.4

Answer 10.5

Answer **B** — Code C, para. 11.2 states:

> Immediately prior to the commencement or re-commencement of any interview at a
> police station or other authorised place of detention, the interviewer should remind the
> suspect of their entitlement to free legal advice and that the interview can be delayed for
> legal advice to be obtained, unless one of the exceptions in paragraph 6.6 applies.

After any break in questioning under caution, the person being questioned must be
made aware they remain under caution. If there is any doubt, the relevant caution
should be given again in full when the interview resumes.

The requirement is to remind the suspect and caution again only where there is
doubt the suspect knows they are still under caution; answers A and C are therefore
incorrect. The fact the suspect is legally represented does not change this; answer D
is therefore incorrect.

Evidence and Procedure, para. 2.10.3

Answer 10.6

Answer **B** — Code C, para. 11.4 states:

> At the beginning of an interview the interviewer, after cautioning the suspect, shall put
> to them any significant statement or silence which occurred in the presence and hearing
> of a police officer or other police staff before the start of the interview and which have
> not been put to the suspect in the course of a previous interview. The interviewer shall
> ask the suspect whether they confirm or deny that earlier statement or silence and if
> they want to add anything.

Code C, para. 11.4A states:

> A significant statement is one which appears capable of being used in evidence against
> the suspect, in particular a direct admission of guilt. A significant silence is a failure or
> refusal to answer a question or answer satisfactorily when under caution, which might,
> allowing for the restriction on drawing adverse inferences from silence, see Annex C,
> give rise to an inference under the Criminal Justice and Public Order Act 1994, Part III.

The refusal was a significant silence as per this definition and can be put to the suspect; answers A, C and D are therefore incorrect.

Evidence and Procedure, para. 2.10.3

Answer 10.7

Answer **A** — It is important not to confuse the duty of disclosure to a person once charged with the need to disclose evidence to a suspect before interviewing them. After a person has been charged, and before trial, the rules of disclosure are clear and almost all material must be disclosed to the defence.

However, this is not necessarily the case at the interview stage of the investigation. There is no specific provision within PACE for the disclosure of any information by the police at the police station, *with the exception of the custody record*. In respect of the provision of a copy of the 'first description' of a suspect it should be noted that Code D (para. 3.1) states that a copy of the 'first description' shall, where practicable, be given to the suspect or his/her solicitor before any procedures under paras 3.5 to 3.10, 3.21 or 3.23 are carried out. In other words, the disclosure requirement is that a copy of the 'first description' shall, where practicable, be given to the suspect or his/her solicitor *before a video identification, an identification parade, a group identification or confrontation takes place*. Therefore, an officer disclosing information to a solicitor at the interview stage (which is taking place in advance of any identification procedures), need not provide the 'first description' of a suspect at that time.

Further, there is nothing within the Criminal Justice and Public Order Act 1994 that states that information must be disclosed before an inference from silence can be made. Indeed, in *R* v *Imran* [1997] Crim LR 754 the court held that it is totally wrong to submit that a defendant should be prevented from lying by being presented with the whole of the evidence against him or her prior to the interview.

So at this stage only the custody record is required to be disclosed; answers B, C and D are therefore incorrect.

Evidence and Procedure, para. 2.10.4.3

Answer 10.8

Answer **B** — Nothing in Code F of the Police and Criminal Evidence Act 1984 Codes of Practice requires the identity of an officer to be recorded or disclosed:

> (b) if the interviewer reasonably believes that recording or disclosing their name might put them in danger.

This is not restricted to terrorism offences; answer C is therefore incorrect.

Note that there is no need for a specific threat to be made against a particular officer; answer D is therefore incorrect.

In these cases, the officers will have their back to the camera and shall use their warrant or other identification number and the name of the police station to which they are attached. Such instances and the reasons for them shall be recorded in the custody record; answer A is therefore incorrect.

Evidence and Procedure, para. 2.10.16

Answer 10.9

Answer **D** — If the suspect makes a complaint regarding his or her treatment since arrest, the interviewing officer must inform the custody officer and follow PACE Code C, para. 12.9, which states:

> If during the interview a complaint is made by or on behalf of the interviewee concerning the provisions of any of the Codes, or it comes to the interviewer's notice that the interviewee may have been treated improperly, the interviewer should:
> (i)   record it in the interview record;
> (ii) inform the custody officer, who is then responsible for dealing with it as in *section 9*.

Note that it is recorded on the interview record, and answer C is therefore incorrect. Code C, para. 9.2 states that 'a report must be made as soon as practicable to an officer of the rank of Inspector or above who is not connected with the investigation'. However, it is not necessary to stop the audio recording; indeed, it should be kept running in accordance with Code E, Note 4E, and answer A is therefore incorrect. Code E, Note 4E also outlines that 'continuation or termination of the interview should be at the discretion of the interviewing officer' and not the custody officer, and therefore answer B is incorrect.

Evidence and Procedure, para. 2.10.4

Answer 10.10

Answer **C** — If there is an equipment failure which can be rectified quickly, e.g. by inserting new recording media, the interviewer shall follow the appropriate procedures that apply to any break in the recordings. When the recording is resumed, the interviewer shall explain what happened and record the time the interview recommences. If, however, it will not be possible to continue recording on that recorder and no replacement recorder is readily available, the interview may continue without being audibly recorded; answers A and B are therefore incorrect. If this happens, the interviewer shall seek the custody officer's authority and not that of an inspector; answer D is therefore incorrect.

Evidence and Procedure, para. 2.10.10.8

Answer 10.11

Answer **B** — The advice concerning visually recorded interviews is contained in Code F of the PACE Codes of Practice. Code F, para. 4.13 states that:

> When a break is to be a short one, and both the suspect and a police officer are to remain in the interview room, the fact that a break is to be taken, the reasons for it and the time shall be recorded on the recording media. The recording equipment may be turned off, but there is no need to remove the recording media. When the interview is recommenced the recording shall continue on the same recording media and the time at which the interview recommences shall be recorded.

Since the officers only intended the break to be a short one, para. 4.13 applies in these circumstances. The previous paragraph states that in these circumstances, the officers *may* turn off the recording equipment, as both the suspect and an officer have remained in the room. Since there is a choice, answers A and C are incorrect. There is no requirement to remove the recording media, because one of the officers and the suspect are still in the room, and there is no likelihood of it being interfered with. Answer D is therefore incorrect.

Whether or not the recording equipment is turned off is a matter for the officers to decide in the circumstances. Further advice is contained in Note 4E, which states that the officer:

> should bear in mind that it may be necessary to satisfy the court that nothing occurred during a break in an interview or between interviews which influenced the suspect's recorded evidence.

Note that in extended breaks, where the suspect leaves the interview room, the recording equipment *must* be turned off and the recording media removed (see para. 4.12).

Evidence and Procedure, para. 2.10.18.4

Answer 10.12

Answer **B** — At the conclusion of an audio-recorded interview the interviewer must sign the label and ask the suspect and any third party present to sign it also.

If the suspect or third party refuses to sign it, an inspector, or if not available a custody officer, shall be called into the interview room and asked to sign it (Code E, para. 4.18).

The inspector is not available so the custody officer should sign the seal and there is no need to seek any authority prior to doing so; answer C is therefore incorrect.

The interviewer has no further part to play where a third party refuses to sign the label; answers A and D are therefore incorrect.

Evidence and Procedure, para. 2.10.18.8

Answer 10.13

Answer **D** — PACE Code C, para. 12.2 provides that a detained person must have a continuous 8-hour 'rest period' while he or she is in detention; this period should normally be at night. The period should be free from questioning, travel or any interruption by police officers in connection with the case. The period may not be interrupted or delayed, except:

- (a) when there are reasonable grounds for believing not delaying or interrupting the period would:
  - (i) involve a risk of harm to people or serious loss of, or damage to, property;
  - (ii) delay unnecessarily the person's release from custody;
  - (iii) otherwise prejudice the outcome of the investigation;
- (b) at the request of the detainee, their appropriate adult or legal representative [this relates to any request not just those that are urgent; answers A and C are therefore incorrect];
- (c) when a delay or interruption is necessary in order to:
  - (i) comply with the legal obligations and duties arising under s. 15;
  - (ii) take action required under s. 9 or in accordance with medical advice.

If the period is interrupted in accordance with (a), a fresh period must be allowed.

Interruptions under (b) and (c) do not require a fresh period to be allowed. The question relates to point (b) and therefore having had 2 hours' rest before being interrupted, 6 more are allocated; answer B is therefore incorrect.

Evidence and Procedure, para. 2.10.4

Answer 10.14

Answer **C** — There is no specific provision within the Police and Criminal Evidence Act 1984 or the Codes of Practice for the disclosure of any information by the police at the police station, with the exception of the custody record and, generally in identification procedures, the initial description given by the witnesses. In respect of the provision of a copy of the 'first description' of a suspect it should be noted that Code D (para. 3.1) states that a copy of the 'first description' shall, where practicable, be given to the suspect or his/her solicitor before any procedures under paras 3.5 to 3.10, 3.21 or 3.23 are carried out. In other words, the disclosure requirement is that a copy of the 'first description' shall, where practicable, be given to the suspect or his/her solicitor before a video identification, an identification parade, a group identification or confrontation takes place. Therefore, an officer disclosing information to a solicitor at the interview stage (which is taking place in advance of any identification procedures) need not provide the 'first description' of a suspect at that time; answers A, B and D are therefore incorrect.

Evidence and Procedure, para. 2.10.4.3

Answer 10.15

Answer **A** — There is nothing within the Criminal Justice and Public Order Act 1994 that states that information must be disclosed by the police prior to interview before an inference from silence can be made; answer B is therefore incorrect. Indeed, in *R* v *Imran* [1997] Crim LR 754 the court held that it is totally wrong to submit that a defendant should be prevented from lying by being presented with the whole of the evidence against him/her prior to the interview. In *R* v *Hoare* [2004] EWCA Crim 784 the Court of Appeal held that the purpose of s. 34 was to qualify a defendant's right to silence rather than to exclude a jury from drawing an adverse inference against a defendant merely because he/she had been advised by his/her solicitor to remain silent, whether or not he/she genuinely or reasonably relied on that advice. Where a defendant had an explanation to give that was consistent with his/her innocence it was not 'reasonable', within the meaning of s. 34(1), for him/her to fail to give that explanation in interview even where he/she had been advised by his/her solicitor to remain silent. Legal advice by itself could not preclude the drawing of an adverse inference; answer D is therefore incorrect. There is a balance to be struck between providing the solicitor with enough information to understand the nature of the case against his/her client and keeping back material which, if disclosed, may allow the suspect the opportunity to avoid implicating him/herself. For instance in *R* v *Thirlwell* [2002] EWCA Crim 286, the Court of Appeal agreed that the solicitor had not been entitled to provisional medical evidence as to possible causes of death in a murder case; answer C is therefore incorrect.

Evidence and Procedure, para. 2.10.4.3

Answer 10.16

Answer **B** — Meal breaks should normally last at least 45 minutes and shorter breaks after two hours should last at least 15 minutes; answers A, C and D are therefore incorrect.

Evidence and Procedure, para. 2.10.4.1

Answer 10.17

Answer **C** — The certified recording media should be capable of having an image of the date and time superimposed upon them as they record the interview; answers A, B and D are therefore incorrect.

Evidence and Procedure, para. 2.10.16.1

Answer 10.18

Answer **A** — Guidance is provided by para. 11.6 of Code C of the Codes of Practice as to when an interview should be concluded. It is important to remember that the interview should not be concluded at the point when there is sufficient evidence to charge or to prosecute but when there is sufficient evidence to provide a realistic prospect of conviction; answers B and C are therefore incorrect. (In *Prouse* v *DPP* [1999] All ER (D) 748 the question was said to be not how much evidence there is but the quality of it.) Once there is enough evidence to prosecute, it may still be necessary to cover those other points in the interview that may be relevant to the defence case and this goes beyond where the officers consider they have asked all relevant questions; answer D is therefore incorrect.

Evidence and Procedure, para. 2.10.10.11

Answer 10.19

Answer **B** — Code C states that a juvenile or person who is mentally disordered or otherwise mentally vulnerable must not be interviewed regarding his/her involvement or suspected involvement in a criminal offence or offences, or asked to provide or sign a written statement under caution or record of interview, in the absence of the appropriate adult unless paras 11.1, 11.18 to 11.20 apply; answer C is therefore incorrect. Paragraph 11.1 outlines that where there was a risk of physical harm to a person an interview without an appropriate adult may take place, this is not dependent on the suspect's solicitor being present; answer A is therefore incorrect. The interview can only take place where a police officer of at least the rank of superintendent considers that delay will lead to the consequences in para. 11.1(a) to (c), and is satisfied the interview would not significantly harm the person's physical or mental state. No mental health professional's advice is needed; answer D is therefore incorrect.

Evidence and Procedure, para. 2.10.3

Answer 10.20

Answer **B** — Section 36 of the Criminal Justice and Public Order Act 1994 provides that inferences can be drawn from an accused's failure to give evidence or refusal to answer any question about any object, substance or mark which may be attributable to the accused in the commission of an offence.

Section 36 states:

(1) Where—
    (a) a person is arrested by a constable, and there is—
        (i)   on his person; or
        (ii) in or on his clothing or footwear; or
        (iii) otherwise in his possession; or
        (iv) in any place in which he is at the time of his arrest, any object, substance or mark, or there is any mark on any such object; and
    (b) that or another constable investigating the case reasonably believes that the presence of the object, substance or mark may be attributable to the participation of the person arrested in the commission of an offence specified by the constable; and
    (c) the constable informs the person arrested that he so believes, and requests him to account for the presence of the object, substance or mark; and
    (d) the person fails or refuses to do so ...

In this scenario the cut would be a mark on his person; as mark is not defined in the legislation this could be 'any' mark; answer D is therefore incorrect. However, since the suspect has in fact accounted for that mark in accordance with s. 36(1)(c) of the 1994 Act, it could not be the subject of a special warning (whether you actually believe the account or not is irrelevant); answer A is therefore incorrect.

'Found by him at a place at or about the time the offence for which he was arrested is alleged to have been committed' relates to the person being found as in s. 37 of the Criminal Justice and Public Order Act 1994, not s. 36. What is important in s. 36 is what is found in the place where he is at the time of his arrest, in this case the knife; answer C is therefore incorrect.

Evidence and Procedure, para. 2.10.2.4

Answer 10.21

Answer **D** — Section 36 of the Criminal Justice and Public Order Act 1994 provides that inferences can be drawn from an accused's failure to give evidence or refusal to answer any question about any object, substance or mark which may be attributable to the accused in the commission of an offence.

Section 36 states:

(1) Where—
    (a) a person is arrested by a constable, and there is—
        (i) on his person; or
        (ii) in or on his clothing or footwear; or
        (iii) otherwise in his possession; or
        (iv) in any place in which he is at the time of his arrest, any object, substance or mark, or there is any mark on any such object; and
    (b) that or another constable investigating the case reasonably believes that the presence of the object, substance or mark may be attributable to the participation of the person arrested in the commission of an offence specified by the constable; and
    (c) the constable informs the person arrested that he so believes, and requests him to account for the presence of the object, substance or mark; and
    (d) the person fails or refuses to do so...
    then if, in any proceedings against the person for the offence so specified, evidence of those matters is given, subsection (2) below applies.

The teeth marks are definitely on his person, however, he did account for the mark (its believability is irrelevant) and as such cannot be given a special warning for it; answers A and C are therefore incorrect.

The property was not found on his person, nor in the place where he was arrested, so it also cannot be subject to a special warning, even if he refuses to account for that property; answers B and C are therefore incorrect.

Evidence and Procedure, para. 2.10.2.4

Answer 10.22

Answer **C** — A jury may draw inferences where a defendant refuses, without good cause, to answer a question properly put. The court must inform the accused that if he or she fails to give evidence, or, being sworn, refuses to answer questions without good cause, the jury may draw such inferences as appear proper from such a failure to give evidence or a refusal to answer any question (*Consolidated Criminal Practice Direction Part IV.44. Defendant's right to give or not give evidence*). Once the defendant becomes a sworn witness, he or she loses the privilege against self-incrimination, and answer A is therefore incorrect. Also, the defendant may be asked questions that tend to incriminate him or her, and answer B is therefore incorrect. So here inferences may be drawn. In *Murray* v *United Kingdom* [1996] 22 EHRR 29 it was held that it would be incompatible with the rights of an accused to base a conviction 'solely or mainly' on his/her silence, or on his/her refusal to answer questions or give evidence in person. The Court of Appeal also held that in cases involving directions under s. 34, the burden of proof remained on the Crown despite the fact that the accused chose to make no comment (*R* v *Gowland-Wynn* [2001] EWCA Crim 2715). Answer D is therefore incorrect.

Evidence and Procedure, para. 2.10.2.6

Answer 10.23

Answer **D** — This question really tests your knowledge of evidence, custody officers procedure and interviews; questions in the national examination also test wide-ranging knowledge. So although this question could be in other chapters, it is in this one as it mostly relates to s. 34 of the Criminal Justice and Public Order Act 1994, inferences from silence.

In relation to the first interview, consider what evidence the police should have disclosed to the solicitor prior to this interview. There is obviously a statutory disclosure duty after charge, however, this is not necessarily the case at the interview stage of the investigation. There is no specific provision within the Police and Criminal Evidence Act 1984 for the disclosure of any information by the police at the police station, with the exception of the custody record and, in identification cases, the initial description given by the witnesses. Further, there is nothing within the Criminal Justice and Public Order Act 1994 that states that information must be disclosed before an inference from silence can be made. Indeed, in *R* v *Imran* [1997] Crim LR 754 the court held that it is totally wrong to submit that a defendant should be prevented from lying by being presented with the whole of the evidence against him or her prior to the interview.

In *R* v *Argent* [1997] Crim LR 346 the court dismissed the argument that an inference could not be drawn under s. 34 of the Criminal Justice and Public Order Act 1994 because there had not been full disclosure at the interview. However, the court did recognise that it may be a factor to take into account, but it would be for the jury to decide whether the failure to answer questions was reasonable. Consider this though: at this stage of the investigation, a few hours after the collision, what actual evidence did the police have? Few, if any, inferences could be drawn, therefore, provided the accused was given an opportunity to give his version of events; answers A and C are therefore incorrect.

In relation to the second interview, Code C of the Police and Criminal Evidence Act 1984 Codes of Practice provides that as soon as a police officer believes that a prosecution should be brought against a suspect and there is sufficient evidence for it to succeed and that the person has said all that he wishes to say about the offence, he shall without delay bring him before the custody officer who is then responsible for considering whether or not he should be charged. Bearing in mind the accused has had no opportunity to comment on the evidence the police have gathered, it would be unfair not to allow him the opportunity to say what he wishes about the offence. In any case, the phrase in Code C is 'sufficient evidence for it to succeed' not 'sufficient evidence to charge' and if the accused's answers led the police to believe that a prosecution is not likely to succeed then that accused must be given the opportunity to say what he wishes; answers B and C are therefore incorrect.

In *R v Flynn* [2001] EWCA Crim 1633, the court held that the police are entitled to conduct a second interview with a suspect, having obtained evidence from their witnesses which was not available in the first interview, and adverse inference could be drawn from the suspect's silence.

Evidence and Procedure, paras 2.10.2.2, 2.10.4.3

Question Checklist

The following checklist is designed to help you keep track of your progress when answering the multiple-choice questions. If you fill this in after one attempt at each question, you will be able to check how many you have got right and which questions you need to revisit a second time. Also available online; to download visit www.blackstonespoliceservice.com.

	First attempt Correct (✔)	Second attempt Correct (✔)
1 Sources of Law and the Courts		
1.1		
1.2		
1.3		
1.4		
1.5		
1.6		
1.7		
1.8		
1.9		
1.10		
1.11		
1.12		
1.13		
1.14		
1.15		
1.16		
2 Instituting Criminal Proceedings		
2.1		
2.2		
2.3		

	First attempt Correct (✔)	Second attempt Correct (✔)
2.4		
2.5		
2.6		
2.7		
2.8		
2.9		
2.10		
2.11		
2.12		
2.13		
2.14		
3 Bail		
3.1		
3.2		
3.3		
3.4		
3.5		
3.6		
3.7		
3.8		
3.9		
3.10		

	First attempt Correct (✔)	Second attempt Correct (✔)
3.11		
3.12		
3.13		
3.14		
3.15		
3.16		
3.17		
3.18		
3.19		
3.20		
4 Court Procedure and Witnesses		
4.1		
4.2		
4.3		
4.4		
4.5		
4.6		
4.7		
4.8		
4.9		
4.10		
4.11		
4.12		
4.13		
4.14		
4.15		
4.16		
4.17		
4.18		
5 Youth Justice, Crime and Disorder		
5.1		
5.2		
5.3		
5.4		
5.5		
5.6		
5.7		

	First attempt Correct (✔)	Second attempt Correct (✔)
5.8		
5.9		
5.10		
5.11		
5.12		
5.13		
5.14		
5.15		
5.16		
5.17		
5.18		
5.19		
6 Exclusion of Admissible Evidence		
6.1		
6.2		
6.3		
6.4		
6.5		
6.6		
6.7		
6.8		
6.9		
6.10		
6.11		
6.12		
6.13		
7 Disclosure of Evidence		
7.1		
7.2		
7.3		
7.4		
7.5		
7.6		
7.7		
7.8		
7.9		
7.10		

	First attempt Correct (✓)	Second attempt Correct (✓)
7.11		
7.12		
7.13		
7.14		
7.15		
7.16		
7.17		

8 Detention and Treatment of Persons by Police Officers

	First attempt Correct (✓)	Second attempt Correct (✓)
8.1		
8.2		
8.3		
8.4		
8.5		
8.6		
8.7		
8.8		
8.9		
8.10		
8.11		
8.12		
8.13		
8.14		
8.15		
8.16		
8.17		
8.18		
8.19		
8.20		
8.21		
8.22		
8.23		
8.24		
8.25		
8.26		
8.27		
8.28		
8.29		
8.30		

	First attempt Correct (✓)	Second attempt Correct (✓)
8.31		
8.32		
8.33		
8.34		
8.35		
8.36		
8.37		
8.38		
8.39		
8.40		
8.41		
8.42		
8.43		
8.44		
8.45		
8.46		

9 Identification

	First attempt Correct (✓)	Second attempt Correct (✓)
9.1		
9.2		
9.3		
9.4		
9.5		
9.6		
9.7		
9.8		
9.9		
9.10		
9.11		
9.12		
9.13		
9.14		
9.15		
9.16		
9.17		
9.18		
9.19		
9.20		
9.21		

Question Checklist

	First attempt Correct (✓)	Second attempt Correct (✓)
9.22		
9.23		
9.24		
9.25		
9.26		
9.27		

10 Interviews

	First attempt Correct (✓)	Second attempt Correct (✓)
10.1		
10.2		
10.3		
10.4		
10.5		
10.6		
10.7		
10.8		

	First attempt Correct (✓)	Second attempt Correct (✓)
10.9		
10.10		
10.11		
10.12		
10.13		
10.14		
10.15		
10.16		
10.17		
10.18		
10.19		
10.20		
10.21		
10.22		
10.23